SPEAK FOR YOURSELF

Book 1

Elizabeth Amy Fein

NEWBURY HOUSE PUBLISHERS, Cambridge
A division of Harper & Row, Publishers, Inc.
New York, Philadelphia, San Francisco, Washington
London, Mexico City, São Paulo, Singapore, Sydney

Library of Congress Cataloging in Publication Data

Fein, Elizabeth Amy.
Speak for yourself.

1. English language--Text-books for foreign speakers.
2. English language--Conversation and phrase books.
I. Title.
PE1128.F36 1984 428.3'4 84-4912
ISBN 0-88377-460-7

Design by Sally Carson
Illustrations by Margie Frem

NEWBURY HOUSE PUBLISHERS
A division of Harper & Row, Publishers, Inc.

Language Science
Language Teaching
Language Learning

CAMBRIDGE, MASSACHUSETTS

First printing: October 1984
Printed in the U.S.A. 5

For My Son, Joshua

ACKNOWLEDGMENTS

First, I would like to thank my mother, Lillian Stockser Fein, without whose help this book could not have been written. Also, I would like to thank Raji Sundararaman for her valuable assistance.

In the development of *Speak for Yourself* from original concept to polished finished product there are several people who deserve mention. I want to thank Karen Davy for pointing me in the direction that the manuscript finally took. Her ideas were provocative and useful. Next, of course, I owe a great debt to Dr. Jan Van Ek's *The Threshold Level for Modern Language Learning in Schools.* I adapted and used directly many of the functions that appear in his seminal book. Special thanks are due to Polly Davis whose *English Structure in Focus* served as my grammar reference book. I also owe a personal debt of gratitude to the two consultants, Linda Ferreira and John Dennis, who helped iron out the kinks in the manuscript. Linda Ferreira in particular, I wish to single out because after reading her comments I always felt helped rather than hurt which is exactly what a good critic should do for an author. Without a doubt, James W. Brown, the ESL editor in charge of *Speak for Yourself,* deserves special thanks. His care, dedication to quality and general enthusiasm helped tremendously make *Speak for Yourself* what it is. Finally, my list of people would not be complete without my mentioning Carol Connor who did an excellent job of typing the manuscript.

Elizabeth Amy Fein

March, 1984

INTRODUCTION

Speak for Yourself is a conversation text for intermediate level ESL students. Book 1 is designed to be used in a six-month conversation course (or in a shorter intensive course) or as a supplemental text in a traditional ESL program.

Speak for Yourself is composed of two volumes. Book 1 contains Part I and Part II; Book 2 contains Part III and Part IV. The structure of *Speak for Yourself* is roughly analogous to a four-act play. The characters, setting, and ideas are all introduced in Part I. Parts II and III state the drama's conflicts, and Part IV presents the resolution of these conflicts. To continue the comparison with a play, each unit in the book can be likened to a mini-scene.

PURPOSE

Speak for Yourself intends to help students improve their speaking skills in English as a Second Language. The text aims to achieve its goal, first and foremost by presenting several models of the spoken language in dialogue form. If students are to learn how to express themselves orally, they need to have a variety of linguistic tools at their disposal. Each unit has four carefully graduated dialogues, culminating with a fifth dialogue the students are asked to write on their own.

Previous texts dealing with spoken English skills depended either too heavily on dialogues or too heavily on grammar instruction. Often students mastered the grammatical concept but did not know how to use it in conversation. Just as often, students who learned a useful expression in a dialogue (e.g., "Want some help?") did not know how to use it in other situations. In other words, the traditional structural, or grammar, approach and the currently popular functional approach were used in isolation with incomplete results.

Speak for Yourself seeks to remedy this problem by providing both structural (grammatical) and functional instruction to help students gain proficiency in speaking English. Important grammatical structures in the dialogues are isolated, taught, and then practiced. Similarly, significant functions (useful expressions) in the dialogues are isolated, explained, and later reinforced.

TEACHING PROCEDURE

There is no one infallible way to teach the material in *Speak for Yourself.* Overall, the teacher should feel comfortable with the text and be familiar with it before beginning the lesson. It is especially important that the teacher know who the characters are and what is happening next. The following sections describe one way to present the material in each unit. But, in the final analysis, the teacher must be his or her own guide. In general, it is advisable that every step of the learning process be carefully monitored and that the students be given sufficient time to do the required work in each unit.

THE OPENING DIALOGUE

Encourage students to guess meanings of new vocabulary, then read the dialogue with the books closed. Have the students open their books, and read it again. Finally, assign different parts to different students for classroom recitation. If there is enough time, see how much the students can remember: write the dialogue on the blackboard with blanks for certain key words. As the students become more adept with this teaching technique, erase more and more of the dialogue.

THE SPIN-OFF DIALOGUE

Begin by explaining any new vocabulary. Next, read the dialogue aloud with the books closed, and then with the books open. Finally, have the students read different roles.

USEFUL EXPRESSIONS

Go over, explain, and practice the expressions and their functions in class. Have the students do the practice exercises either in class or for homework.

STRUCTURES

Teach or review the grammar structures, and have the students do the practice exercises either in class or for homework.

TRANSFER

Essentially these exercises transfer the opening and spin-off dialogues to other situations. This is a crucial part of the text, so it is vital that the students do these two exercises correctly. In the beginning, both the transfers should be done in class under careful teacher supervision. Later on, one or both of them may be done as homework.

MAKING A CONVERSATION

Like the preceding transfers, it is important that the students are successful in doing this exercise. Once the students feel that they can make satisfactory original conversations, they are on their way to becoming proficient in English communication skills. You may want the students to read some of their conversations aloud in class as a stimulus for greater motivation.

TOPICS FOR DISCUSSION

The students have already worked with several dialogues—passively and then actively—based on the theme of the unit. They have also studied key grammar structures, useful expressions and their functions, and the new vocabulary. Now have the students express themselves orally on a variety of topics. During the classroom discussion be supportive and foster an atmosphere of tolerance for other people's ideas.

Before you begin *Speak for Yourself,* I would like to add one last word as a "bon voyage." So far this Introduction has described *Speak for Yourself* in purely pedagogical terms. Granted, the text has its serious sides as well as its light-hearted sides. But above everything else, I would like both teachers and students to view *Speak for Yourself* as a book to be enjoyed—as a human comedy showing the frailties, frustrations, and joys common to us all. And I sincerely hope that you—teachers and students alike—have as much fun in using the text as I did in writing it.

CONTENTS

Acknowledgments *iv*
Introduction *v*
The Characters *xii*

PART I

	GRAMMATICAL STRUCTURES	FUNCTION	USEFUL EXPRESSIONS Example
UNIT 1 Settling In *page 2*	**A. Separable 2-Word Verbs** **B. Present Modal—CAN (Possibility)**	Directing Others Making a Request Making a Suggestion Expressing Possibility	Move it . . . Could you . . . Let's . . . How about taking . . . We can . . .
UNIT 2 Meeting a New Neighbor *page 8*	**A. Present Perfect Tense + *Just*** **B. Past Tense + *Just*** **C. The *Get* Passive**	Offering Assistance Greetings Expressing Gratitude Making an Introduction Responding to an Introduction	Can I give you a hand? Want some help? Can I help you? Do you want some help? Hi./Hello. How do you do? Thanks./Thank you. I'm . . . I live . . . This is . . . Nice to/Glad to meet you.
UNIT 3 Having Breakfast *page 16*	**A. The Present Modal—SHOULD (Advisability)** **B. Indirect Speech** **C. Noun Modifiers**	Greetings Asking about a Desire Refusing an Offer Giving Advice Making a Suggestion Asking for Information . . .	Good morning./Morning. Do you want . . . Would you like . . . No, thanks./No, thank you. You should . . ./ You shouldn't . . . How about + noun Do you know . . .
UNIT 4 Walking around the Neighborhood *page 24*	**A. Exclamations** **B. Verb + Infinitive**	Giving a Warning Asking about One's Well-being Expressing Uncertainty Expressing a Desire Expressing an Exclamation	Look out!/Watch out! Are you okay?/all right? I guess . . . I want/would like/'d like . . . What a . . . !

	GRAMMATICAL STRUCTURES	FUNCTION	USEFUL EXPRESSIONS Example
UNIT 5 **Making Up One's Mind** *page 30*	**A. Present Modal—MIGHT (Possibility in the Present or in the Future** **B. Preposition + Gerund (Phrase)** **C. Verb (Phrase) + Gerund** **D. Idioms + Gerund (Phrases) as Complements**	Expressing Preference Asking about Preference Asking about Certainty Stating One Does Not Know	I'd rather (not) . . . Would you rather . . . ? Which would you rather . . . ? Are you sure . . . ? I don't know . . .
UNIT 6 **Checking Up on Another Person** *page 36*	**A. Future—Be Going to** **B. Present Continuous** **C. with Future Meaning** ***Too* and *Very***	Expressing Intention Inquiring about Intention Expressing Obligation/Necessity Giving a Warning Taking Leave	I'm going to . . . Are you going to . . . ? I don't have to . . . Don't . . . See you later./So long.
UNIT 7 **On the Telephone** ***Talking to the Information Operator*** *page 42*	**A. *Say* and *Tell*** **B. *Help* and *Let***	Making a Request Expressing Gratitude Allowing Someone (or Something) to Complete an Act Asking Someone to Wait Taking Leave	Can you . . . Thank you (very much). Let me . . ./Let the . . . Just a minute./Hold on. Good-bye./Bye-Bye./Bye. Have a nice day.
UNIT 8 **On the Telephone (B)** ***Talking to a Health Club Receptionist*** *page 48*	**A. Infinitives after Nouns or Indefinite Pronouns** **B. More 2-Word Verbs**	Greeting People on the Telephone Expressing Agreement Expressing Approval Expressing Interest	Hello. Good morning/afternoon/evening. (name of establishment) Yes./Certaintly./Sure. Good. (That sounds) very good. I'm interested in + noun
UNIT 9 **In the Library** *page 54*	**A. Present Tense—Passive Voice** **B. Present Perfect Tense with *Already* and *Yet***	Attracting Attention Expressing Surprise Making an Apology Responding to an Apology Making a Suggestion	Excuse me . . . What a + noun I'm sorry./Sorry. That's all right. Why don't you . . . ?
UNIT 10 **Saying Hello to a Friend** *page 60*	**A. Adjective + Infinitive** **B. Adverbs of Manner and Quantity after Verbs and Direct Objects**	Expressing Result Expressing Certainty Greetings Expressing Pleasure Expressing Intention	. . . , so . . . I thought (that) . . . I think (that) . . . How are you?/doing?/ How's everything going? I like . . . You will . . .

PART II

	GRAMMATICAL STRUCTURES	FUNCTION	USEFUL EXPRESSIONS Example
UNIT 11 At a Housewarming Party (A) *Making Small Talk* page 68	**A. Adjective Comparatives** **B. Negative Infinitives**	Expressing Pleasure Expressing Obligation/ Necessity Giving a Negative Answer Correcting a Negative Statement	This is . . ./It's . . . I must . . . No, I didn't. No, I didn't. But I *did* . . .
UNIT 12 At a Housewarming Party (B) *Eating Too Much* page 74	**A. *A little* and *A few*** **B. Units of Measure with Mass Nouns** **C. Verb + Gerund**	Expressing Inability Expressing Displeasure Making an Offer Accepting an Offer or Invitation	I can't . . . I don't like . . . Can I get you . . . ? Yes, please./Thank you.
UNIT 13 At a Housewarming Party (C) *Making a Date* page 82	**A. Verb + Infinitive** **B. Adverbs of Frequency**	Expressing Certainty and Uncertainty Inviting Others Seeking Permission Giving Permission	I think (that) . . ./I don't think so. Would you like to . . . ? Can I . . . ?/May I . . . ? Yes, you can/may.
UNIT 14 Borrowing Some Sugar page 88	**A. Inseparable 2- and 3-Word Verbs** **B. Present Modal—WOULD without Understood Condition (*If*-Clause)** **C. Present Modal—WOULD with Improbable Condition (Infinitive plus Phrase)**	Expressing Agreement When Handing Someone Something Responding to Gratitude Asking for Information (Tag Question) Giving an Affirmative Answer	Sure./Certainly. Here./Here you are. You're welcome. You're from . . . , aren't you? Yes, I am.
UNIT 15 A Father and Son Chat page 94	**A. Verbs of Perception—*See, Hear,* etc.** **B. Reflexive Pronouns**	Inquiring about One's Well-being Expressing Agreement Expressing Indifference Correcting a Negative Statement	What's the matter?/What's wrong? Right./That's right. I don't care./It doesn't matter. You *do* care.

	GRAMMATICAL STRUCTURES	FUNCTION	USEFUL EXPRESSIONS Example
UNIT 16 Making an Appointment with the Doctor *page 100*	A. **Present Modal—SHOULD (Expectation in the Present or in the Future)** B. **Modal—COULD (Possibility in the Present or in the Future)** C. **Future Adverbial Clauses of Time**	Asking for Confirmation Asking about Certainty Expressing Obligation Expressing Certainty	We can . . . *You can?* Do you think (that) . . . ? We have to . . . I think so.
UNIT 17 In the Examining Room *page 106*	A. **Gerunds and Gerund Phrases as Subjects** B. **Count Nouns and Mass Nouns without *The***	Expressing Fear or Worry Asking for Approval Expressing Inability	I'm worried (that) . . . Is it all right that . . . ? Is that all right? Is this okay? You won't be able to . . .
UNIT 18 At a Bar *page 112*	A. **Conditional with an *If*-Clause (Present Time)** B. **Future Noun Clauses after *Wish***	Expressing a Desire Expressing Disapproval Making a Request	I'd like . . . I shouldn't be . . . We shouldn't have come . . . Please take . . .
UNIT 19 Meeting Someone by Chance *page 118*	A. ***Unless*** B. **Noun Clauses as Direct Objects with and without *That***	Responding to a Greeting Asking about Ability Expressing Ability	How are things (with you)? Fine./Okay. Can you . . . ? I can./I can see.
UNIT 20 Saying Good Night *page 124*	A. **Direct Objects and Indirect Objects** B. ***Enough***	Reminding Someone Forgetting Responding with a Short Question Taking Leave	Remember . . . I forgot to . . . Oh, have you? Good night.

These are called garden apartments because each building has only a few floors. Often, however, there are no gardens. Because the buildings are usually small, the neighbors in each building frequently get to know one another. Mr. and Mrs. Spock and their daughter have just moved into Apartment 2A.

THE CHARACTERS

The Spocks

These are the Spocks. Steve Spock is a personnel specialist working for the state civil service. His wife, Paula, used to be a computer programmer. Now she's a homemaker. Lisa is one year old.

Soon the Spocks will meet their neighbors: Carol Wright and her daughter Brenda, Frank and Judy Climo and their sons Dan and Ricky, and Harry Mullens.

The Wrights

Mrs. Wright and her fifteen-year-old daughter, Brenda, live in the apartment across the hall from the Spocks. Carol Wright, who is divorced, works as a secretary in a bank. Brenda is a high school student.

Mr. Mullens

Mr. Harry Mullens lives in the apartment below the Wrights. He's a retired widower. Harry Mullens used to be a coach for a football team. Now he's especially interested in physical fitness.

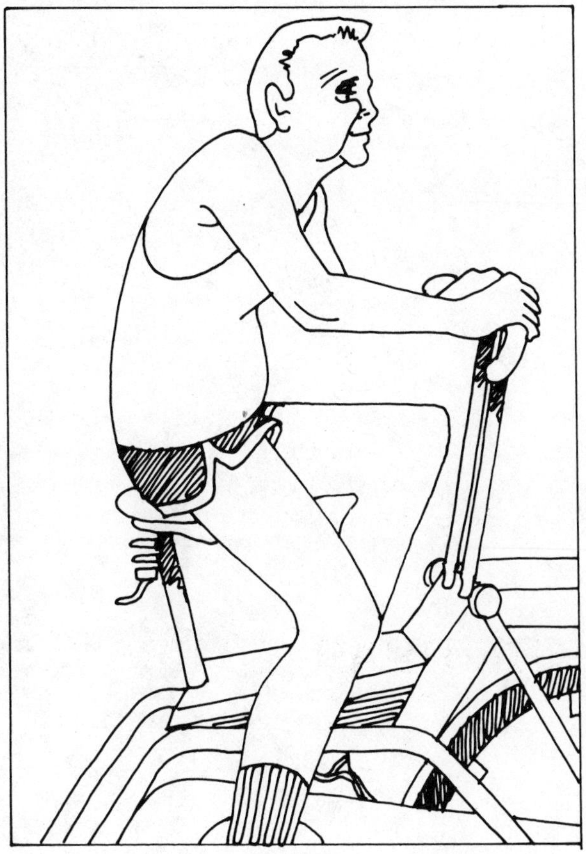

The Climos

Mr. and Mrs. Climo and their two sons live in the apartment below the Spocks. Frank Climo owns a secondhand clothing store. His wife, Judy, is a homemaker. Their older son, Dan, is eighteen, and he's in his first year of college. Their younger son, Ricky, is sixteen, and he's in his third year of high school.

PART I

Part I begins in October. It is autumn in the Northeast of the United States. There are four distinct seasons in this region of the country. Many people say that autumn is the most beautiful season because the leaves on the trees change to brilliant colors and then fall to the ground. Today is one of those perfect days when the sun is bright, and the air is cool and fresh.

UNIT 1

Settling In

Paula: This is definitely the right place for the sofa. Could you put the rug in front of it?

Steve: Sure . . . How's this?

Paula: Hm . . . Okay, I think . . . Just straighten it out a little.

Steve: Is this all right?

Paula: Yes. It's fine just like that.

Steve: Hon, after we hang up the pictures, let's go out for a walk.

Paula: That's a great idea. And we can bring Lisa along too.

SPIN-OFF DIALOGUE

Paula: This is the right spot for the couch, all right. Could you put the area rug in front of it?

Steve: Like this?

Paula: Hm . . . Let me see . . . Just move it a little closer to the couch.

Steve: Is this enough?

Paula: Yeah. It's fine now.

Steve: After we hang up the curtains, how about taking a walk around the neighborhood?

Paula: That's a wonderful idea. And we can bring Lisa along with us.

USEFUL EXPRESSIONS

Directing Others:	*Move* it a little closer. (imperative form of verb)
Making a Request:	*Could you* put the rug in front of it?
Making a Suggestion:	*Let's* go out.
	How about tak*ing* a walk? (verb + ing)
Expressing Possibility:	We *can* bring Lisa.

VOCABULARY

NOUNS
area
couch
curtains
idea
neighborhood
picture
rug
sofa
spot
walk

ADJECTIVES
close
enough
fine
great
right
wonderful

ADVERBS
definitely
in front of
just (=exactly, only)

IDIOMS AND PHRASES
all right
bring along
hang up
hon (short form of honey)
Let me see.
okay
put
settle in
straighten out
take a walk
yeah (yes)

PRACTICE I

1. **Choose the correct word(s) to complete these sentences.**

example: Could you **to put/put/putting** it here?
Could you put it here?

1) How about **take/took/taking** a walk?
2) Just **to straighten/straighten/straightened** it out a little.
3) Steve and Paula can **brought/to bring/bring** Lisa along.

4) Let's **hang/hung/hanging** up the pictures.

5) Could you **moving/move/moved** the rug a little closer?

6) How about **putting/to put/put** it in front of the sofa?

7) The baby can **going/go/to go** out.

8) **To put/Putting/Put** it in the right spot.

2. Put these words in the correct order to make sentences.

example: her they take can along .
They can take her along.

1) like it's just that fine .

2) curtains up hang the .

3) the you front put in rug of could it ?

4) going for out walk about a how ?

5) couch it closer little the move a to .

6) Lisa can we along bring .

7) is the definitely place the for right this sofa .

8) around walk let's the take a neighborhood .

STRUCTURES

A. Separable 2-Word Verbs

Hang up *Take down* *Put away*	**the picture**		*Hang* *Take* *Put*	**the picture**	*up.* *down.* *away.*
Bring along	**Lisa.**		*Bring*	**Lisa**	*along.*

When the direct object is a noun, we put it *after* the 2-word verb or *between* the verb and the adverbial particle.

Hang *Take* *Put*	**it**	*up.* *down.* *away.*
Bring	**her**	*along.*

When the direct object is a pronoun, we put it *between* the verb and the adverbial particle.

B. Present Modal—CAN (Possibility)

Subject +	*can* +	Verb (Base Form)
We	*can*	**bring Lisa along.**
Lisa	*can't*	**stay alone in the apartment.**

A modal is an auxiliary verb that we use to modify the main verb in some way. Modals express expectation, possibility, advisability, and conditions that are understood, improbable, or otherwise contrary to fact.

PRACTICE II

1. Change the direct objects from nouns to pronouns.

examples: Let's take John along.
Let's take <u>him</u> along.
Let's take along John.
Let's take <u>him</u> along.

1) They took down the curtains.
2) She hung the curtains up again.
3) The Spocks can bring their daughter along.
4) Straighten the area rug out.
5) After we hang up the picture, let's go out.
6) How about taking along my friend and me?
7) Put the magazines away.
8) Take down the mirror.

2. Read the following paragraph. Then fill in the blanks with the correct items from the list.

in	along	can	right	a	in front of
go	room	fine	hang	it	apartment

The Spocks have just moved into <u>Apartment</u> (1) 2A. They are settling ____________ (2) now. Steve and Paula moved the sofa to the ____________ (3) place for it in the living ____________ (4). Paula asked Steve to put the area rug ____________ (5) the sofa. The rug looks ____________ (6) there except Paula wants Steve to straighten ____________ (7) out. Steve suggests they ____________ (8) out for a walk after they ____________ (9) up the pictures. Paula thinks that's ____________ (10) great idea and that they ____________ (11) bring their baby daughter, Lisa, ____________ (12) with them.

TRANSFER

1. You are helping Paula Spock decorate her living room. Read the dialogue first; then fill in the blanks with appropriate phrases or sentences.

Paula: The wall unit is a good place for the TV. Could you put it on one of the shelves?

Student: ____________ . ____________________________ ?
(Say, "Sure." Ask how this is.)

Paula: Let me see . . . I think it's too high up. Put it on a lower shelf.

Student: ____ ?
(Ask if it's okay here.)

Paula: Yeah. It's fine there.

Student: Well, we're finished now.
____ ?
(Suggest a change of scene. Begin with how about.*)*

Paula: That's a terrific idea.

2. You are helping Paula Spock move the table in her kitchen. Read the dialogue first; then fill in the blanks with appropriate phrases or sentences.

Paula: Could you put the table near the window please?

Student: ____________ . ____________________________ ?
(Say, "Sure." Ask if this is all right.)

Paula: Hm . . . It's okay. Just move it out a little.

Student: ____ ?
(Ask if this is enough.)

Paula: Yes. It's perfect.

Student: ____
(Invite Paula to take a break. Begin with how about.*)*

Paula: That's a great idea. And we can take Lisa with us.

MAKING A CONVERSATION

Write a conversation with your partner. Choose one of the following situations, or try one of your own.

1. You are studying with a classmate. When you are almost finished, one of you suggests going out somewhere together.

2. You are cleaning your apartment or house with a family member or friend. When you finish a very difficult task, one of you suggests relaxing in some way.

TOPICS FOR DISCUSSION

1. How do you think Paula and Steve Spock feel after moving into their new apartment? Was Steve's suggestion to go out for a walk a good idea? Why? Have you ever moved?

2. Do you think Steve, Paula, and Lisa Spock are all settled in now? Why not? How long do you think it takes to feel settled in after moving to a new place? What does it depend on? If you have moved, how long did it take *you*?

UNIT 2

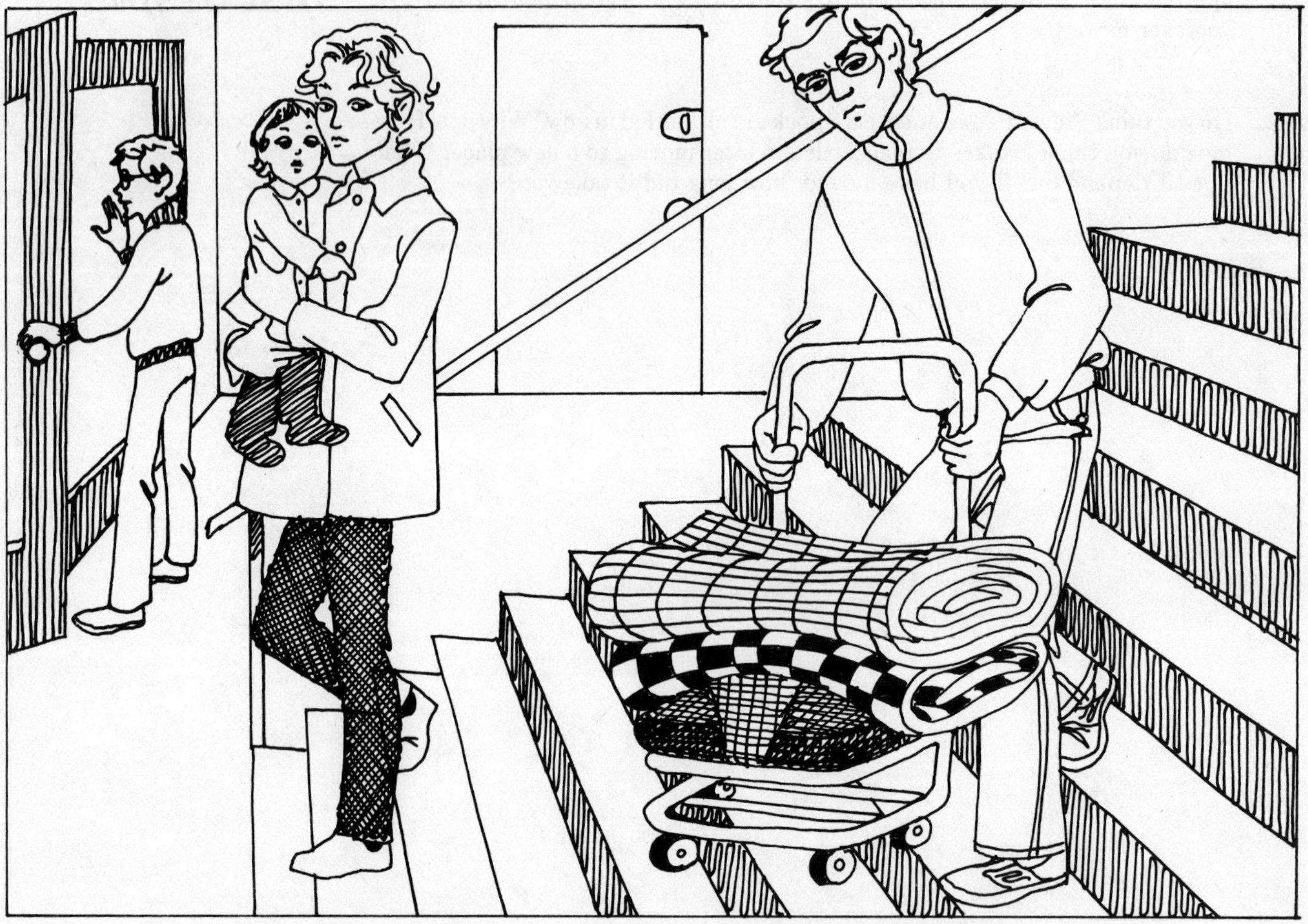

Meeting a New Neighbor

Ricky: Hi. Can I give you a hand?

Steve: Yeah. Thanks.

(Ricky helps Steve carry the baby's stroller down the stairs. Then they put it down on the floor.)

Ricky: Have you just moved in?

Steve: Yes. Just yesterday afternoon.

Ricky: Well, welcome to the building. Uh . . . I'm Ricky Climo. I'm a junior* in high school.

Steve: Nice to meet you, Ricky. I'm Steve Spock. I just got transferred to this city. This is my wife, Paula.

Paula: Hi. And this is Lisa.

Ricky: Hello, Lisa.

*A junior is a third-year high school student.

SPIN-OFF DIALOGUE

Ricky: Hi. Want some help?

Steve: Yes. Thanks.

(Ricky takes the front end of the stroller and helps Steve carry it to the bottom of the stairs. Then they put it down.)

Ricky: Did you just move in?

Steve: Yeah. Just yesterday afternoon.

Ricky: Wow! Uh . . . I'm Ricky Climo. I live in 1A.

Steve: Glad to meet you. I'm Steve Spock. We just moved into 2A, right above you. This is my wife, Paula.

Paula: Hi, Ricky. And this is Lisa.

Ricky: Hi, Lisa.

USEFUL EXPRESSIONS

Offering Assistance: *Can I give you a hand?* (informal)
Want some help? (informal)
Can I help you?
Do you want some help?

Greetings: *Hi.*
Hello.
How do you do? (formal)

Expressing Gratitude: *Thanks.* (informal)
Thank you. (formal)

Making an Introduction: *I'm* Ricky Climo (name). I *live in 1A* (additional information).
This is Lisa.

Responding to Introduction: *Nice to meet you.*
Glad to meet you.

VOCABULARY

NOUNS	VERBS	ADVERBS
baby	carry out	just (very recent past)
bottom	got (get)	right (=exactly)
building	live	above
circumstance	meet	
end	move in	
floor	put down	
front	transfer	
help		
high school		
junior		
neighbor		
stairs		
stroller		
student		
wife		

ADJECTIVES
awkward
glad
nice
social

IDIOMS AND PHRASES
at ease
Can I give you a hand?
get transferred, etc. (get + past participle =passive voice)
Glad to meet you.
Nice to meet you.
Welcome.
Well.
Wow!

PRACTICE I

1. Fill in the blanks with the correct word.

example: Can I give you a hand?

1) Nice ______________ meet you.
2) Do you want ______________ help?
3) I ______________ Ricky Climo.
4) How do you ______________ ?
5) ______________ I help you?
6) This ______________ Lisa.
7) I live ______________ 1A.
8) ______________ some help?

2. Carry out the following instructions.

example: Introduce yourself. I'm Edward Blake. I live in New York.

1) You see a friend on the street. Greet him.
2) Someone is carrying a suitcase with difficulty. Offer assistance.
3) You want one friend of yours to meet another friend. Introduce one friend to the other, and then vice versa.
4) Your teacher explains the meaning of a difficult word in English. Express gratitude.
5) Introduce yourself to a student near you.
6) The student introduces himself/herself.
7) A tourist is lost in your city. Offer assistance.

8) You meet a famous American politician. Greet him/her.
9) A good friend pays for your coffee. Express gratitude.
10) The student next to you doesn't understand the homework assignment. Offer assistance.

STRUCTURES

A. Present Perfect Tense + *Just*

Have/Has + **Just** + Past Participle
I've **just** *moved in.*

Yes/no question: *Have* you **just** *moved* in?

She*'s* **just** *locked* the door.
He*'s* **just** *helped* them.
They*'ve* **just** *gone out.*

We use the present perfect for an indeterminate time in the past. We add **just** when it's the very recent past.

B. Past Tense + *Just*

Just + Past Tense
We **just** *moved in.*

Yes/no question: *Did* you **just** *move in*?

I **just** *saw* them.
He **just** *put down* the stroller.
The baby **just** *smiled.*

We sometimes use **just** with the past tense when it means the very recent past.

C. The *Get* Passive

Get + Past Participle
I *got* *transferred.*

One box *got lost* in the move.
A vase *got broken.*
A table *got scratched.*
The mail *gets delivered* around 11 o'clock.

We use the *get* passive with informal speech to emphasize a recent action. (However, we use the idioms *get engaged, get married,* and *get divorced* with any time expression.)

PRACTICE II

1. Answer these questions with *just* using the cue word(s).

example: When did you see Mark? (we) (yesterday)
We just saw him yesterday.

1) When did he help her with her work? (last Monday)
2) When did they lock the door? (five minutes ago)
3) When did Paula meet her neighbor? (this morning)
4) When did you clean the shelves? (I) (last week)
5) When did the Spocks move into their new apartment? (yesterday afternoon)
6) When did the cool weather begin? (two days ago)
7) When did you finish the assignment? (we) (at 4:00)
8) When did he lose his keys? (this afternoon)

2. Change these sentences from the regular passive voice to the *get* passive.

example: The little girl was lost in the big store.
The little girl got lost in the big store.

1) Steve was transferred to another city.
2) Many workers in that factory were laid off recently.
3) This desk was scratched in the move.
4) My friends were engaged last month.
5) When will they be married?
6) He was lost in New York City.
7) When she dropped her pocketbook, the mirror in it was broken.
8) All of our difficulties were straightened out.

3. Change these sentences from the past to the present perfect tense.

examples: They just locked the door.
They've just locked the door.

She just took down the picture.
She's just taken down the picture.

1) I just smiled at them.
2) She just was outside.
3) You just lost your key.
4) Mr. and Mrs. Spock just moved into the apartment above 1A.

5) He just saw the TV program.
6) We just opened the boxes.
7) Tom just finished.
8) They just looked at the new building.

4. Make sentences from these words.

example: You have just move in.
You've just moved in.

1) He got transfer .
2) The Spocks have just meet a new neighbor .
3) She just introduce Lisa .
4) I got lose .
5) He have just give them a hand .
6) A few glasses got break .
7) We have just get a new wall unit .
8) You just see her .

TRANSFER

1. You are a new student at Ricky Climo's high school. He sees you looking for something. He thinks you are lost. You are looking for the auditorium because your sister has asked you to wait for her there. Read the dialogue first; then fill in the blanks with appropriate phrases or sentences.

Ricky: You look lost. Can I help you?

Student: ________ . ______________________ ?
(Say, "Yes." Ask him where the auditorium is.)

Ricky: The entrance is right over there . . . Uh, are you a new student?

Student: ______________________________ .
(Tell him today is your first day.)

Ricky: Oh! Well, I hope everything went okay. Uh. . . I'm Ricky Climo. I'm a junior.

Student: ______________________________ .
(Respond to the introduction.

______________________________ .
Introduce yourself.

______________________________ .
Your sister, Mary, walks up to you. Introduce her to Ricky.)

Ricky: Hi.

2. You are a new employee at Steve Spock's office. This morning you're having some trouble operating the coffee machine. Steve offers to help you. You are with another employee, named Bill. Read the dialogue first; then fill in the blanks with the appropriate phrases or sentences.

Steve: Want some help?

Student: ______________ . ______________________________________ ?
(Say, "Yeah, thanks." Ask him how to operate the coffee machine. He shows you how to operate the machine.)

Steve: Did you just start working here?

Student: ____ .
(Say, "Yes, just a couple of days ago.")

Steve: This is my first week here, too. I'm Steve Spock. I'm a personnel specialist.

Student: ____ .
(Respond to the introduction.

____ .
Introduce yourself.

____ .
Introduce Bill.)

Steve: Nice to meet you.

MAKING A CONVERSATION

Write a conversation with your partner. Choose one of the following situations, or try one of your own.

1. You are at a party. Another guest is looking for a place to sit down. You find him/her a chair. Then you introduce yourself and the other person introduces himself/herself. The spouse or a friend of the other guest comes by, and the other guest introduces him/her.

2. You are at the theater, waiting for a friend and his brother. You don't know his brother. When the two arrive, you and your friend greet each other. Then your friend introduces his brother. You have already bought tickets for everyone. So you give them their tickets. They thank you.

TOPICS FOR DISCUSSION

1. Do you think Steve and Paula Spock were glad to meet Ricky Climo? Why?

2. How did Ricky help the Spocks? Have you given someone a hand recently? What did you do?

3. When you meet someone for the first time, do you feel a little awkward like Ricky or do you feel socially at ease? Does it depend on certain circumstances? If so, which ones?

UNIT

3

Having Breakfast

Frank: Good morning, dear.

Judy: Good morning. Do you want eggs for breakfast?

Frank: No, thanks. I'm late. I'll just have some coffee.

Judy: You should have more than that. How about some toast?

Frank: All right. Do you know if Dan went to the store?

Judy: He said he was going there when he went out half an hour ago.

Frank: Good.

SPIN-OFF DIALOGUE

Frank: Good morning.

Judy: Morning. Do you want pancakes for breakfast?

Frank: No. I don't have time. I'll just have some orange juice and a cup of coffee.

Judy: You should have something more substantial. How about an English muffin at least?

Frank: Okay. Do you know if Dan went to the store?

Judy: When he left, he said he was going there to open up.

Frank: I'm glad he remembered.

USEFUL EXPRESSIONS

Greetings: *Good morning.*
Morning. (very informal)

Asking about a Desire: *Do you want* eggs for breakfast?
Would you like eggs for breakfast?

Refusing an Offer: *No, thanks.* (informal)
No, thank you.

Giving Advice: *You should* have more than that.
You shouldn't eat so much.

Making a Suggestion: *How about* some toast?
(+ noun)

Asking for Information about Something or Someone: *Do you know* if Dan went to the store? (something)
Do you know the name of the store? (something)
Do you know the owner of the store? (someone)
Do you know what time the store closes? (something)

VOCABULARY

NOUNS
advisability
breakfast
coffee
companion
cup
dinner
egg
juice
muffin
orange
pancake
programmer
store
toast

VERBS
help out
left (leave)
open up
remember
want
went out (go out)

ADJECTIVES
concerned
half
late
substantial

IDIOMS AND PHRASES
ago (half an hour ago)
dear (n)
I don't have time.
something in particular

PRACTICE I

1. Put these words in the correct order to make sentences.

example: about pancakes some how ?
<u>How about some pancakes?</u>

1) you eggs breakfast want for do ?
2) know time what do he you left ?
3) substantial something you have should more .
4) the Dan if to do store know went you ?
5) muffin how English about an ?
6) orange you have a should of juice glass .
7) breakfast doesn't for he want pancakes .
8) that more have than should you .

2. Carry out the following instructions.

example: Ask if your friend wants cereal for breakfast.
<u>Do you want cereal for breakfast?</u>
or, <u>Would you like cereal for breakfast?</u>

1) Ask if your classmate knows all his/her neighbors.
2) It's 9:00 A.M. Greet a member of your family.
3) Your friend is getting too fat. Give him advice.
4) A relative is at your home. It's very hot. Suggest something cool to drink.
5) Ask if your spouse/roommate wants to go to a movie tonight.
6) It's 11:00 A.M. Greet the owner of a store.
7) Your breakfast companion doesn't like eggs. Suggest something else.
8) Ask if your classmate knows the answer to the last question.
9) Your co-worker is often nervous. She drinks six cups of coffee every day. Give her advice.
10) Ask if your friend wants to go out for a walk.

STRUCTURES

A. Present Modal—SHOULD (Advisability)

Subject +	*should* +	Verb (Base Form)
You	*should*	**have** more than that.
You	*should not*	**eat** too much.

B. Indirect Speech

Direct	Indirect
He *said,* I'*m going* there."	He *said* (that) he *was going* there.
She *said,* "I *want* some milk."	She *said* (that) she *wanted* some milk.
They *said,* "We *did* it."	They *said* (that) they'*d done* it.
They *said,* We'*ve done* it."	(they + *had*)
You *said,* "I *can go.*"	You *said* (that) you *could go.*
We *said,* "We'*ll be* early."	We *said* (that) we'*d be* early. (we + *would*)
I *said,* "I *should eat* some eggs."	I *said* (that) I *should** *eat* some eggs.

C. Noun Modifiers

Noun + Noun	=	Noun Modifier + Noun
juice made from *oranges*	=	*orange juice*
muffins made from *corn*	=	*corn muffins*
a *cup* for *coffee*	=	a *coffee cup*

PRACTICE II

1. Answer the following questions with *should.*

example: Frank Climo sometimes gets up late. When should he get up?
He should get up on time.

1) You have a test tomorrow. What should you do tonight?
2) Judy can't see well without her glasses. What should she do?
3) The old man and his wife are very tired from their walk. What should they do?
4) You want to speak English fluently. What should you do?
5) It's raining outside. What should the man take with him when he goes out?
6) A tourist just arrived in your city. Where should she go first?
7) You are late for an appointment. What should you do?
8) Some little children are playing near the street. Where should they play?

**Should* is the same in direct and indirect speech.

2. Change these sentences from direct speech to indirect speech.

example: She said, "I know Nancy."
She said (that) she knew Nancy.

1) He said, "I'm glad."
2) The little boy said, "I can hang it up."
3) Mrs. Climo said, "You should eat more."
4) I said, "I'll make some tea."
5) They said, "We're leaving now."
6) She said, "Dan went to the store."
7) I said, "I always get up at seven o'clock."
8) He said, "I've just had breakfast."

3. Fill in the blanks with a noun modifier.

example: You broke the coffee cup.

1) We cleaned the ____________ table.
2) That family drinks a lot of ____________ juice.
3) Paula Spock was a ____________ programmer.
4) Mr. Climo owns a ____________ store.
5) Dan Climo is a ____________ student.
6) His brother, Ricky, is a ____________ ____________ student.
7) Where are the ____________ muffins?
8) I don't watch many ____________ programs.
9) Steve Spock is a ____________ specialist.
10) You had some trouble with the ____________ machine.

TRANSFER

1. Frank Climo has just come to your house/apartment for a meeting. Read the dialogue first; then fill in the blanks with appropriate phrases or sentences.

Frank: Hi.

Student: ____________. ________________________?
(Say, "Hi." Ask him if he'd like some cheese and crackers.)

Frank: No, thanks. I'll just have some nuts.

Student: ________________________________?
(Offer him a piece of fruit. Begin with how about.*)*

Frank: Okay. Do you know if everybody has arrived yet?

Student: ____.

(Say, Yes, everyone is here.

____.

We can begin the meeting very soon.")

Frank: Good.

2. Frank is an old friend of your family. He's staying at your house/apartment. When he got up this morning, he wasn't feeling hungry. He's just walked into your kitchen. Read the dialogue first; then fill in the blanks with appropriate phrases or sentences.

Frank: Good morning.

Student: ____.

(Say, "Good morning."

____?

Ask him if he wants bacon and eggs for breakfast.)

Frank: No, thank you. I'm not very hungry.

Student: ____

(Suggest a cup of coffee and a corn muffin.

____?

Begin with how about.)

Frank: All right. Do you know if my wife called last night after I went to bed?

Student: ____

(Say, "Yes." Tell him she called and she said, "I want him to call

____.

me back.")

MAKING A CONVERSATION

Write a conversation with your partner. Choose one of the following situations, or try one of your own.

1. A co-worker from the office comes to your home in the afternoon. You offer him/her a snack. He/she only wants a little. You offer something else and he/she accepts. Then he/she asks you a question using "know."

2. You are sitting down at the table for a meal with a family member. You ask him/her if he/she wants something in particular on the table. He/she refuses and gives a reason. You advise him/her to eat more and suggest something else to eat. The other person accepts it, and then changes the subject and asks you a question with "know."

TOPICS FOR DISCUSSION

1. Did Frank have a good breakfast? Why not? What did he have to eat? What did you have for breakfast this morning?

2. Do you have breakfast every day? If you don't, why do you skip breakfast? If you eat breakfast, what do you have for breakfast?

3. In general, do you eat well? If you don't, how should you change your eating habits?

4. Is Judy Climo concerned about her family? Why do you think so?

5. Does Dan help his father out in his secondhand clothing store? How do you know? Do you have a job? If you do, where do you work?

UNIT 4

Walking around the Neighborhood

Steve: Hey Paula! Look out! *(A small branch lightly grazes Paula's face.)*

Paula: Ugh!

Steve: Are you okay?

Paula: Yeah . . . I guess I wasn't looking where I was going. I just wanted to see how Lisa was doing.

Steve: How is she doing?

Paula: Just fine . . . Do you want to cross the street?

Steve: *(Steve looks around.)* Okay . . . Isn't it a beautiful day?

Paula: Yes, it is. And the leaves are really pretty . . . Look at that tree over there.

Steve: Yeah. And look at that one up the street.

SPIN-OFF DIALOGUE

Steve: Paula! Watch out! *(A twig grazes Paula's cheek.)*

Paula: Ugh!

Steve: Are you all right?

Paula: Yes. I guess I'd better look where I'm going. I just wanted to see how Lisa was.

Steve: How is she?

Paula: Just fine . . . Do you want to walk up the hill?

Steve: Okay . . . What a beautiful day!

Paula: Oh, yes. And the leaves are really gorgeous . . . Look at the tree on the corner.

Steve: Yeah. And look at the one in front of the white house.

USEFUL EXPRESSIONS

Giving a Warning:	*Look out!* *Watch out!*
Asking about One's Well-being:	*Are you okay?* *Are you all right?*
Expressing Uncertainty:	I *guess* I wasn't looking where I was going.
Expressing a Desire:	I *want* to see how Lisa is. I *would like . . .* I'*d like . . .*
Expressing an Exclamation:	*What a* beautiful day!

VOCABULARY

NOUNS
branch
cheek
corner
face
hill
house
intersection
leaf (pl. leaves)
scenery
street
tree
twig

VERBS
cross
graze
guess
had better
look at
walk

ADJECTIVES
beautiful
gorgeous
pretty
small

IDIOMS AND PHRASES
Hey!
Look out!
Ugh!
Watch out!

PRACTICE I

1. Put the words in the correct order to make sentences.

example: lovely a what street !
What a lovely street!

1) all you right are ?
2) pretty are leaves the really .
3) better guess where I'd I'm look I going .
4) day beautiful a what !
5) wanted Lisa I see how doing to was just .
6) everybody is okay ?
7) was looking I wasn't going guess I where I .
8) like the around we walk would neighborhood to .

2. Read the following paragraph. Then fill in each blank with the correct item from the list.

face	around	out	was	okay	wanted
walk	what a	guess	at	tree	gorgeous

Steve, Paula, and Lisa Spock went for a ___walk___ (1). When Paula bent down to look ________ (2) Lisa, Steve yelled, "Watch ________ (3)!" But it was too late. A ________ (4) branch grazed Paula's ________ (5). Steve asked her if she was ________ (6). Paula answered, "Yes. I ________ (7) I wasn't looking where I was going." Paula ________ (8) to see how Lisa was. Steve and Paula looked ________ (9) at the ________ (10) leaves on the trees. Steve thought it ________ (11) a beautiful day, so he said, "________ (12) beautiful day!"

STRUCTURES

A. Exclamations

What	+	Mass Noun		
What		weather!		
What	+	Adjective	+	Mass Noun
What		nice		weather!
What	+ *a* +	Singular Count Noun		
What	a	night!		

What	+ *a*	+ Adjective	+	Singular Count Noun
What	a	beautiful		night!
What	+	Adjective	+	Plural Count Noun
What		beautiful		nights!

We use the article *a* in exclamations which contain singular count nouns.

B. Verb + Infinitive

They { *want* / *would like* / *hope* } **to look at** the scenery.

We use an infinitive object after some verbs. Other verbs that take infinitive objects include: *decide, promise,* and *try.*

PRACTICE II

1. Change these sentences to exclamations.

examples: The lake is pretty.
What a pretty lake!

The information is useful.
What useful information!

The days are long.
What long days!

1) The pictures are gorgeous.
2) The weather is bad.
3) The houses are beautiful.
4) The idea is wonderful.
5) The air is fresh.
6) The questions are hard.
7) The rug is old.
8) The neighborhood is nice.

2. Make sentences from these cue words.

example: (we) (decided) (take a walk)
We decided to take a walk.

1) (he would like) (study English)
2) (we hope) (get transferred)
3) (you tried) (remember its name)
4) (Paula wanted) (know) (how Lisa was doing)
5) (I decided) (wait at the corner)
6) (they'd like) (get married)
7) (I hope) (see you again)
8) (she promised) (be more careful)

TRANSFER

1. You are walking with Steve Spock at a busy intersection. Without looking, you start to cross the street. A car is moving toward you. Read the dialogue first; then fill in the blanks with appropriate phrases or sentences.

Steve: Hey _____________! Look out!
(your name)

Student: ____!
(Say, "Ugh!")

Steve: You should look where you're going.

Student: ____.
(Say, "Yeah."

____.
Tell him you were thinking about something important you're doing now.)

Steve: How is it coming along?

Student: ____.
(Say, "Very well.")

Steve: *(Steve looks around him and at the sky.)* What a beautiful night!

Student: ____.
(Say, "Yes . . . And it's so clear. Look at all the stars.")

2. You are bicycle riding with Steve Spock in a small town. You turn your bicycle into the entrance of a street. Steve sees a hole in the street right in front of you. Read the dialogue first; then fill in the blanks with appropriate phrases or sentences.

Steve: _____________! Watch out!
(your name)

(You almost fall off your bicycle as you just miss the hole in the street.)

Student: ______________________________________!

(Say, "Ugh!")

Steve: Are you okay?

Student: ______________________________________.

(Say, "Yes." Tell him you just wanted to see what was

______________________________________.

down that street.)

Steve: What's down there?

Student: ____________. ______________________________?

(Say, "A little square." Ask him if he wants to go see it.)

Steve: Okay . . . Isn't this an interesting town?

Student: ______________________________________.

(Say, "Yes, it is.")

MAKING A CONVERSATION

Write a conversation with your partner. Choose one of the following situations, or try one of your own.

1. You and a friend are in a small boat on a lake. Another small boat comes very close, and you yell out a warning. The boat just misses you.

2. You are at a friend's house. While you are walking down the stairs to the basement, your friend warns you that the bottom step is broken. But you step on it anyway.

TOPICS FOR DISCUSSION

1. What are some other situations when people say, "Look out!" or, "Watch out!"? Have you said one of these expressions recently? What happened? Did someone say it to you? Was it said in time?

2. Do you think the Spocks are enjoying their walk? Why? Or why not? What beautiful things are they admiring?

   Do you enjoy looking at the beauty of nature? Where do you like to go? What things do you like to look at?

3. Is autumn your favorite season of the year? Why? If not, which season do you think is the most beautiful? Why?

UNIT 5

Making Up One's Mind

Mrs. Wright: Would you rather go to the post office and then go to the shopping mall or go to the shopping center first?

Brenda: I don't know.

Mrs. Wright: Well, I'd rather go to the post office first and then spend the rest of our time shopping.

Brenda: I don't feel like shopping.

Mrs. Wright: What do you feel like doing?

Brenda: Studying. Maybe I'll go to the library.

Mrs. Wright: Are you sure you don't want to come with me?

Brenda: Yes. But thanks for asking.

SPIN-OFF DIALOGUE

Mrs. Wright: Which would you rather do—go to the post office and then the shopping mall or go to the shopping center first?

Brenda: I don't know.

Mrs. Wright: Well, I'd rather go to the post office first and then go shopping.

Brenda: I don't want to go shopping.

Mrs. Wright: What do you want to do?

Brenda: Maybe study. I might go to the library.

Mrs. Wright: Are you sure you don't want to look at some winter coats at the mall?

Brenda: Yes.

USEFUL EXPRESSIONS

Expressing Preference:	I'*d rather* go to the post office. (positive) (*would*) I'*d rather not* go to the hospital. (negative) (*would*)
Asking about Preference:	*Would* you *rather* go shopping first? *Which would* you *rather* do—go to the post office and then go shopping or go to the shopping center first?
Asking about Certainty:	*Are* you *sure* you don't want to come with me?
Stating One Does Not Know:	*I don't know* Charles

VOCABULARY

NOUNS
coat
library
mall
post office
rest
shopping center
thanks
winter

ADJECTIVE
sure

ADVERBS
first
then

IDIOMS AND PHRASES
feel like + (verb + ing)
make up one's mind
spend time + (verb + ing)
would rather + verb (base form)

PRACTICE I

1. Fill in the blanks with the correct word.

example: Mrs. Wright would rather go shopping.

1) Are you ____________ you don't want to go to the mall?

2) Brenda doesn't ______________ everyone in her building.

3) ______________ would they rather have—coffee or tea?

4) I ______________ rather go to the post office first.

5) Would you ______________ stay in or go out?

6) ______________ he sure that he is right?

7) What would you rather ______________—go swimming or go dancing?

8) I'd rather ______________ go dancing. I don't feel like it.

2. Carry out the following instructions.

example: Ask your classmate if he/she is sure that he/she understands.
Are you sure you understand?

1) You prefer to read the newspaper. Express your preference.
2) Your friend likes to go to concerts and to the movies. Ask him what his preference is.
3) State you don't know Mary's address.
4) Ask your acquaintances if they are sure the post office is open.
5) State you don't know your friend's husband.
6) Your teacher likes to drive a car and ride a bicycle. Ask him/her what his/her preference is. Use "which."
7) Mrs. Wright prefers to take Brenda to the shopping center. Express her preference.
8) However, Brenda prefers to study. Express her preference.

3. ***Correct or Incorrect.*** **If the following statements are correct, say, "That's correct." If they are incorrect, say, "That's incorrect." Then make the statements correct.**

examples: I prefer to take a walk. I'd rather take a walk. That's correct.

He prefers not to wash the dishes. He'd rather wash the dishes.
That's incorrect. He'd rather not wash the dishes.

1) Can you introduce me to those people? I don't know them.
2) They prefer not to stay home. They'd rather stay home.
3) We want to know if you are certain of your answer, so we ask, "Are you sure of your answer?"
4) He likes to receive letters more than write them. He'd rather write letters.
5) I prefer to sit on the sofa. I'd rather sit on the sofa.

STRUCTURES

A. Present Modal—MIGHT (Possibility in the Present or in the Future)

I *might* go to the library.

B. Preposition + Gerund

Thanks *for* **asking.**

C. Verb (Phrase) + Gerund (Phrase)

He doesn't *feel like* **working.**
He *feels like* **going to the movies.**
He *enjoys* **seeing Westerns.**

D. Idioms + Gerund (Phrases) as Complements

We *spent our time* **talking.**
We *had trouble* **making a decision.**
You *were busy* **finishing your report.**
They *were having fun* **taking a break.**

PRACTICE II

1. **Make two sentences with *might* and *should* and the cue words.**

example: Bill is tired. (watch TV) (go to bed)
He might watch TV. He should go to bed.

1) She feels like taking a break. (go outside) (continue working)
2) I can't make up my mind which relative to see. (visit my Cousin Paul) (see my grandparents)
3) Joseph and I are sometimes late for class. (be late today) (be on time)
4) Brenda's mother likes those dresses. (buy one of them) (wait until her next paycheck)
5) You studied very hard for the last test. (get an "A") (study hard for every test)
6) The car isn't working very well. (It/break down) (I/take it to a mechanic)
7) He's drinking too much at the party. (get sick) (stop)
8) The weather changes here frequently. (It/rain this afternoon) (I/listen to the weather forecast on the radio)

2. Fill in the blanks with the appropriate gerund from the list.

studying	making	buying	doing
asking	shopping	going	

Mrs. Wright wanted to go the post office and then spend the rest of her time shopping (1). She enjoys ____________ (2) things for herself and her daughter. She asked her daughter to go along with her. Brenda sometimes enjoys ____________ (3) to the mall very much. But today she wasn't sure what she felt like ____________ (4). She had trouble ____________ (5) up her mind. When she finally made her decision, she said that she felt like ____________ (6). Brenda is a polite girl. So she thanked her mother for ____________ (7) her to go shopping with her.

TRANSFER

1. You are visiting Carol Wright. She wants to take you sightseeing. Read the dialogue first; then fill in the blanks with appropriate phrases or sentences.

Mrs. Wright: Would you rather go to the old church and then to the Indian museum or go to the Indian museum first?

Student: ____________________________________.
(Say that you don't know.)

Mrs. Wright: Well, I'd rather go to the old church first and then spend the rest of our time looking at everything in the museum.

Student: ____________________________________.
(Say that you don't feel like sightseeing.)

Mrs. Wright: What do you feel like doing?

Student: ____________________________________.
(Say, "Taking a walk outdoors." Suggest going to the park.
____________________________________.
Begin with, "Let's.")

Mrs. Wright: Are you sure you don't want to go to the museum today?

Student: ____________________________________.
(Say, "Yes, but thank you for offering to take me.)

2. You are at a shopping mall with Brenda. She wants to show you a few of the places there. Read the dialogue first; then fill in the blanks with appropriate phrases or sentences.

Brenda: Would you rather go the pizza place for a snack and then go to the bookstore or go to the bookstore first?

Student: ____________________________________.
(Say that you don't know.)

Brenda: I'd rather go to the pizza place first and then spend the rest of our time looking at books.

Student: ______________________________________.
(Say that you don't want to stay at the shopping mall.)

Brenda: What do you want to do?

Student: ______________________________________.
(Say, "Go home." You need to do some ironing.)

Brenda: Are you sure you don't want to stay at the shopping center?

Student: ______________________________________.
(Say, "Yes, but thanks for asking.")

MAKING A CONVERSATION

Write a conversation with your partner. Choose one of the following situations, or try one of your own.

1. You are with a friend or a family member on a rainy afternoon. Ask him/her which of two rainy day activities he/she would rather do first—play cards or do a jigsaw puzzle.

2. You are shopping in a department store with a friend or family member. Ask him/her which department he/she would like to go to first—the sportswear department or the jewelry department.

TOPICS FOR DISCUSSION

1. Do you feel like studying right after school? Can you study right away, or do you have to do something else before you can begin to study?

2. What do you like to spend a lot of time doing? What don't you like to spend a lot of time doing?

3. Did Brenda have trouble making up her mind? How do you know? Do you generally make up your mind quickly or slowly? When does it take you a long time to make up your mind?

UNIT

6

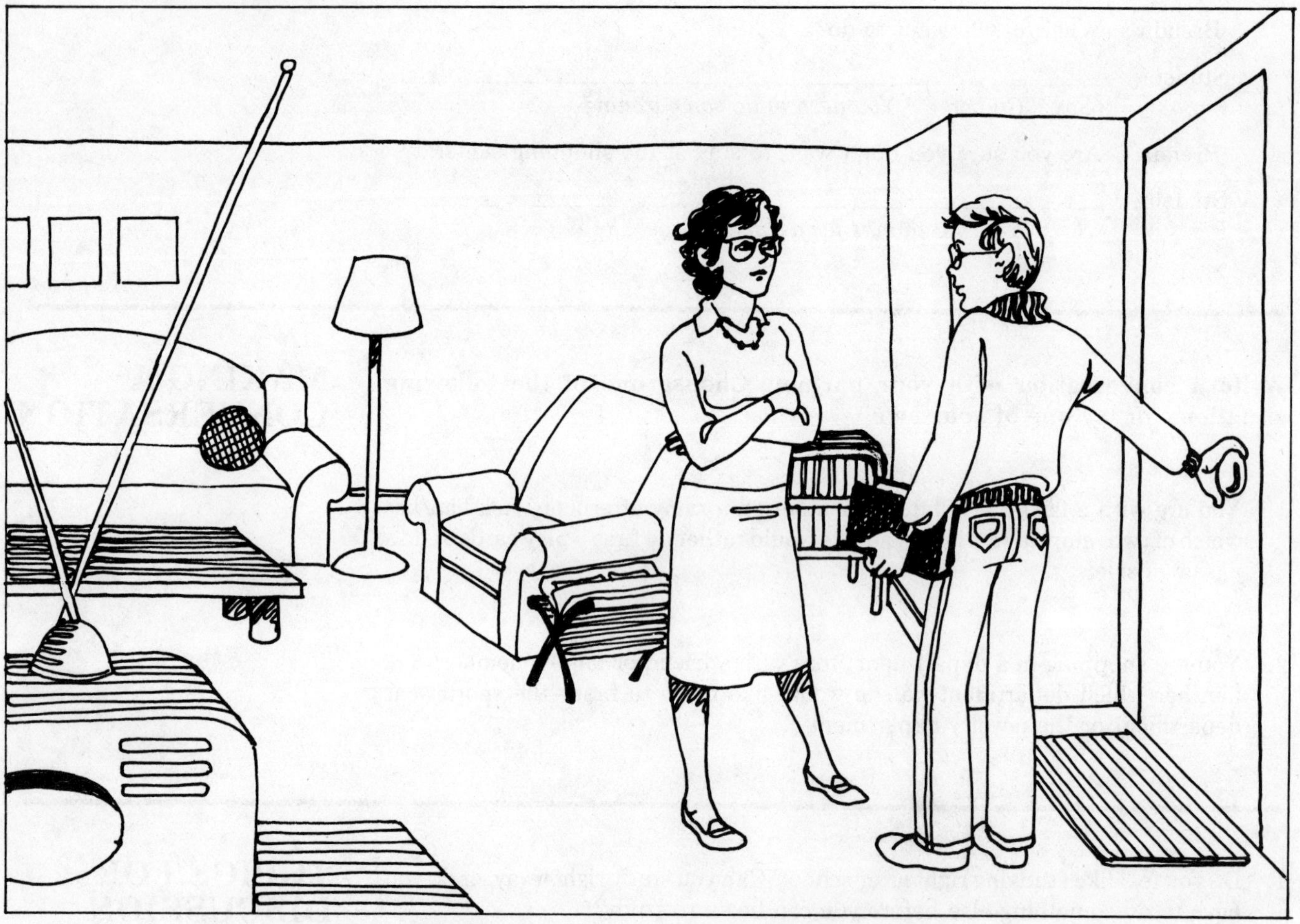

Checking Up on Another Person

Mrs. Climo: Who were you talking with outside?

Ricky: Our new neighbors.

Mrs. Climo: Our new neighbors?

Ricky: Yes. Mr. and Mrs. Spock and their baby daughter. They just moved into the Gordons' old apartment.

Mrs. Climo: Oh, is that so? . . . Say, Ricky, are you going to help out your father in the store today?

Ricky: No. Dad said I didn't have to. I'm going to the library.

Mrs. Climo: Well, don't forget to be home by six. We're having dinner then.

Ricky: I won't forget. See you later.

SPIN-OFF DIALOGUE

Mrs. Climo: Who were you talking to outside the building?

Ricky: Mr. and Mrs. Spock.

Mrs. Climo: Who?

Ricky: They're our new neighbors. They just moved into 2A with their baby daughter.

Mrs. Climo: Really! . . . Ricky, are you going to help out in the store today?

Ricky: No, Dad said I didn't have to work today. I'm going to the library.

Mrs. Climo: Well, don't stay out too late. We're having dinner at six.

Ricky: Don't worry. I'll be home before then. So long.

USEFUL EXPRESSIONS

Expressing Intention:	I'*m going to* go to the library. (+ verb)
Inquiring about Intention:	*Are* you *going to* help out? (+ verb)
Expressing Obligation/Necessity:	I don't *have to* work. (+ verb)
Giving a Warning:	*Don't* stay out too late.
Taking Leave:	*See you later.* (informal) *So long.* (informal)

VOCABULARY

NOUNS
apartment
daughter
dinner
home
person

ADJECTIVES
another
old

VERBS
check up on
forget
help out
said (say)
stay out
talk
worry

IDIOMS AND PHRASES
Is that so?
make one's train, plane
Really!
Say, . . .
See you later.
So long.

PRACTICE I

1. Choose the correct word(s) to complete the sentences.

example: Don't **forgetting/to forget/forget** to do it.
Don't forget to do it.

1) Are you going **help out/to help out/helping out** in the store?
2) So **long/longer/longest.**
3) He **doesn't/don't/do** have to come home before six.
4) **No/don't/did** worry.
5) I'm **to go/going/gone** to stay out all afternoon.
6) See you **late/later/latest.**
7) Dinner doesn't **has to/having to/have to** be ready at five-thirty.
8) Mrs. Climo is going **to read/read/reading** a good book.

2. Put these words in the correct order to make sentences.

example: early didn't to he have home be .
He didn't have to be home early.

1) you later see .
2) the I'm to library going .
3) six forget to home don't be by .
4) today Ricky have work didn't to .
5) worry don't . before home I'll then be .
6) your are help going you out father to ?
7) home stay to have doesn't she .
8) they're have six dinner to going at .

STRUCTURES

A. Future—*Be Going to*

To Be Going to	+	main Verb
Dan'*s going to*		*help out* in the store.
Ricky'*s going to*		(*go* to) the library.
They'*re going to*		*have* dinner at six.

When the main verb is *go,* it is often omitted after the *to be going to* verb phrase.

B. Present Continuous with Future Meaning

We'*re having* }
We'*re eating* } dinner at six.
We'*re serving* }

The present continuous tense can be used for the future.

C. *Too* and *Very*

The train left at 9:15. She got to the station at 9:20 and missed the train.
= She came *too* late.

He got to the station at 9:12 and got on the train. = He came *very* late, but he made his train.

Too has a negative connotation. *Very* is an adverb intensifier.

PRACTICE II

1. **Fill in the blanks with the correct form of the *to be going to* verb phrase + the main verb in parentheses or the present continuous tense of the main verb.**

Ricky isn't going to help out (help out — not) his father in his clothing store. Ricky is going (go) to the library. His brother Dan ____________ (help) his father. Mr. Climo and Dan ____________ (work) at the store until 5:30. Mrs. Climo ____________ (have) a quiet day. She ____________ (go out — not). The Climos ____________ (have) dinner at six. But Mrs. Climo ____________ (cook — not). She ____________ (heat up) leftovers from yesterday's dinner.

2. **Answer the questions with *too* or *very* and the cue word (s).**

example: Why can't you wear your coat? (small)
Because it's too small.

Why is Linda carrying the heavy box? (strong)
Because she's very strong.

1) Why did he drink two glasses of water? (thirsty)
2) Why are they smiling? (happy)
3) Why didn't the student finish the exam? (long)
4) Why is she a good driver? (careful)
5) Why can't you hang up the curtains? (short)

6) Why can't he ask her to dance? (shy)
7) Why do you like that book? (interesting)
8) Why can't she wear makeup? (young)

TRANSFER

1. **While you are shopping at the supermarket, you see Ricky. He's with another person. Later you ask him who it was. Read the dialogue first; then fill in the blanks with appropriate phrases or sentences.**

Student: ______________________________?
(Ask who Ricky was talking with at the supermarket.)

Ricky: Cesar Valdez.

Student: ______________________________?
(Say, "Who?")

Ricky: He's Dan's friend from Peru. He's going to Hudson Community College.

Student: ______________________________?
(Ask, "Is that so?" Then ask Ricky if he's going to
______________________________?
the chess club this afternoon.)

Ricky: No, I'm going to the library.

Student: ______________________________
(Tell him not to miss the tournament if he
______________________________.
can help it.)

Ricky: I won't. See you later.

2. **You see Ricky playing soccer with two other boys. Later, you ask him who he was playing with. Read the dialogue first; then fill in the blanks with appropriate phrases or sentences.**

Student: ______________________________?
(Ask who Ricky was playing soccer with.)

Ricky: Tim and Larry Burke.

Student: ______________________________?
(Say, "Who?")

Ricky: They're my cousins. They're visiting for the day.

Student: ______________________________.
(Say, "Oh."
____
Ask Ricky if he's going to soccer practice Monday after school.
______________________________?
Begin with "Say,")

Ricky: No, the coach said I didn't have to. I'm going to exercise a little at home though.

Student: ____ .
(Tell him not to forget to go to practice Wednesday afternoon.)

Ricky: Don't worry. I'll be there. So long.

MAKING A CONVERSATION

Write a conversation with your partner. Choose one of the following situations, or try one of your own.

1. You see a friend walking down the main street of your town or city with a very beautiful woman. Some time later you and your friend are talking, and you ask him who it was. Then you ask him if he's going back to the office.

2. You see a friend or a family member in a very animated conversation with a couple in a line at a movie theater. Later you ask him/her who he/she was talking with. Then you ask him/her if he/she is going to take the bus home.

TOPICS FOR DISCUSSION

1. Do you think Mrs. Climo is "nosey"—that she wants to know about everyone else's business? Or do you think she has a healthy curiosity? Do you know any nosey people? What do they like to do?

2. Ricky isn't going to help out his father in the store today. Where is he going? Are you going any place after school? Where? What are you going to do there?

3. When are the Climos having dinner? When are you having dinner tonight? Where and with whom are you having it? Describe the circumstances.

UNIT
7

On the Telephone (A)

Talking to the Information Operator

Harry:	Can you please tell me the phone number for Volner Health Club?
Operator:	How do you spell that?
Harry:	V – O – L – N – E –R.
Operator:	Did you say "N" as in Nancy or "M" as in money?
Harry:	"N" as in Nancy.
Operator:	Thank you. It's 260–0472.
Harry:	Just a minute. Let me get a pencil . . . What was that again?
Operator:	It's 260–0472. *(He writes the number down.)*

Harry: Thank you. Good-bye.

Operator: Have a nice day.

SPIN-OFF DIALOGUE

Harry: What's the phone number for the Volner Health Club?

Operator: How is that spelled?

Harry: V – O – L – N – E – R.

Operator: Did you say "N" as in "Nancy"?

Harry: Yes.

Operator: I have a Volner Health Club on Beekman Street.

Harry: That's it. Let me just get a pen . . . Okay.

Operator: The number is 260–0472. *(He writes it down.)*

Harry: Thank you very much. Good-bye.

Operator: Have a nice day.

USEFUL EXPRESSIONS

Making a Request: *Can* you tell me the phone number?

Expressing Gratitude: *Thank you.* (formal)
Thank you very much.

Allowing Someone (or Something) to Complete an Act: *Let me* get a pencil.
Don't start to drive yet. *Let the motor* run.

Asking Someone to Wait: *Just a minute.*
Hold on.

Taking Leave: *Good-bye.* (formal)
Bye-bye. (informal)
Bye. (informal)
Have a nice day.

VOCABULARY

NOUNS
club
customer
health
information
money
number
operator
pen
pencil
phone

VERBS
connect
let
say
spell
write down

IDIOMS AND PHRASES
Have a nice day.
Hold on.
Just a minute.
on the telephone

PRACTICE I

1. Fill in the blanks with the correct word(s).

example: Have a nice day.

1) Before Mr. Mullens hung up, he said, "______________."
2) Let me ______________ a pen.
3) ______________ you for giving me the information.
4) Harry Mullens was talking on the telephone to his friend. Before he hung up, he said, "______________."
5) ______________ you tell me the phone number?
6) Have ______________ nice day.
7) ______________ I use your dictionary?
8) In the middle of Mary's telephone conversation, the doorbell rang. She said, "Hold ______________."

2. Carry out the following instructions.

example: Take leave of a young child on the telephone.
Bye-bye.

1) A lawyer gives you some good advice. Express gratitude.
2) Ask your friend on the telephone to wait.
3) Seek permission from the school secretary to use the telephone.
4) Take leave of a family member on the telephone.
5 Ask an acquaintance to tell you the name of a good health club.
6) A telephone operator helps you out. Express gratitude.
7) You are not sure of a telephone number. Seek permission from a friend to call Information to check it.

STRUCTURES

A. *Say* and *Tell*

Did you *say* **"N"**?	I *said* **the answer.**
Did you *tell* ***her?***	I *told* ***them*** the **answer.**

We use *say* with direct objects that are things.
We use *tell* with indirect objects that are people.

B. *Help* and *Let*

Verb +	Agent +	Verb (Base Form)
Help	**him**	***find*** the telephone book.
Let	**him**	***look up*** the number himself.

PRACTICE II

1. Choose the correct word to complete these sentences.

examples: I **said/told** "please."
I said "please."

They **said/told** us a story.
They told us a story.

1) Did she **say/tell**, "Come at seven o'clock"?
2) Can you please **say/tell** me the club's address?
3) Has he **said/told** them everything?
4) She wants to **say/tell** George about her conversation.
5) I **said/told** it three times.
6) They should **say/tell** their mother.
7) Did you **say/tell** "lose" or "loose"?
8) We **said/told** her but not him.

2. Fill in the blanks with the correct form of the verb in parentheses.

examples: Harry Mullens wanted to call (call) the Volner Health Club.
You helped them finish (finish).

1) They let us ____________ (use) their office.
2) Would you like ____________ (be) a member of that club?
3) We tried ____________ (understand).
4) My friend can help me ____________ (carry) the bags.
5) Did you promise ____________ (call) your parents on Sunday?
6) Let me ____________ (get) you something to eat.
7) The Information Operator helped Mr. Mullens ____________ (find) a telephone number.
8) She decided ____________ (tell) them the truth.

TRANSFER

1. You call up the billing department of a large company. Read the dialogue first; then fill in the blanks with appropriate phrases or sentences.

Student: ______________________________
(Tell the customer service representative you have a question

______________________________.

about your last bill.)

Customer Service Representative: What's your name please?

Student: ______________________________.
(Say your last name.)

Customer Service Representative: How do you spell that?

Student: ______________________________.

Customer Service Representative: Did you say __________ or __________?
(one letter) *(another letter)*

Student: ______________________________.

Customer Service Representative: Hold on, please . . . Thank you for waiting. I'll connect you with Mr. Tinsley. He handles your account.

Student: ______________________________.
(Express gratitude.)

2. You call up a bus company to find out their afternoon schedule for buses going to Hampton. Read the dialogue first; then fill in the blanks with appropriate phrases or sentences.

Student: ______________________________?
(Ask when they have buses going to Hampton this afternoon.)

Ticket Agent: Did you say Hampden or Hampton?

Student: ______________________________.

Ticket Agent: Thank you. We have buses leaving at 12:40, 2:15, 4:25, and 5:30.

Student: ______________________________.
(Say, "Just a minute."

______________________________.

Allow yourself to get a pen. Ask for permission.

______________________________?

Ask the ticket agent to repeat what he said.)

Ticket Agent: The times are 12:40, 2:15, 4:25, and 5:30.

Student: ______________________________.
(Express gratitude.)

Ticket Agent: Good-bye.

MAKING A CONVERSATION

Write a conversation with your partner. Choose one of the following situations, or try one of your own.

1. You want to know when a certain movie begins. So you call up the movie theater and ask when the movie is playing. A theater employee tells you the times but you can't remember them. You ask the theater employee's permission to wait while you get a pencil to write the information down.

2. You call up the bank about your checking account. You think there's a mistake on your last statement. The bank officer asks you your name which is Mr./Mrs./Ms. Wojcik. Then he/she asks you how to spell it.

TOPICS FOR DISCUSSION

1. What telephone number did Harry Mullens ask the Information Operator for? Did he get it? What was it? Have you called Information recently? If you have, did you remember the telephone number, or did you write it down?

2. What did the operator ask Harry to spell? Do people often ask you to spell your name? Why? What do you ask other people to spell?

3. Was the Information Operator polite to Harry? How do you know? What is the special way telephone operators say "good-bye" in the U.S.? What do people say in your country (1) when they answer the telephone? and (2) when they take leave?

4. What do you think Harry is going to do next? Why do you think he wants the phone number for a health club? Answer with "might."

UNIT 8

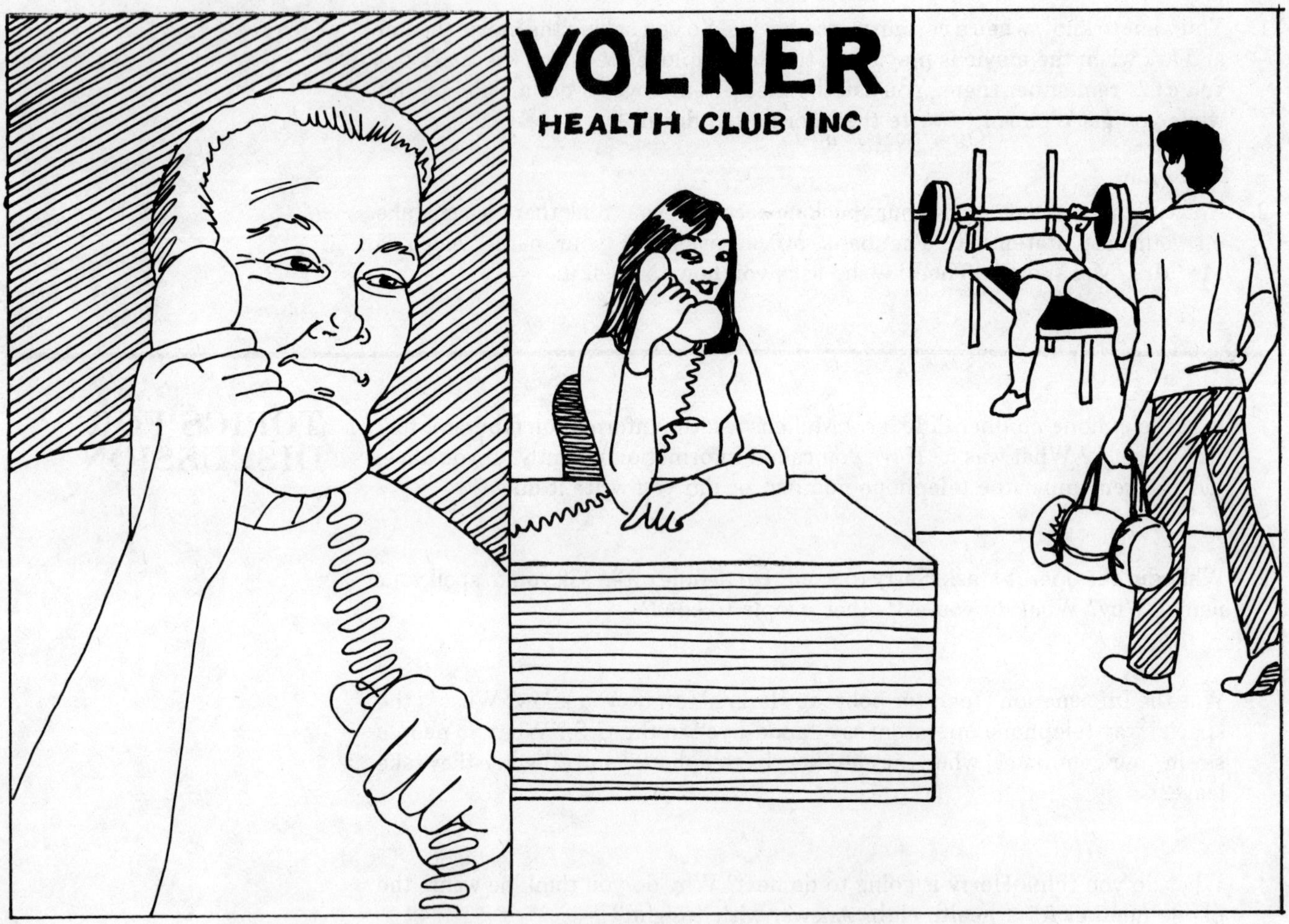

On the Telephone (B)

Talking to a Health Club Receptionist

Receptionist:	Good morning. Volner Health Club.
Harry:	Hello. Could you give me some information about your health club?
Receptionist:	Certainly. What would you like to know?
Harry:	What kind of facilities do you have?
Receptionist:	We have an Olympic-sized swimming pool, a track for jogging and a weight room.
Harry:	That sounds very good. How much does it cost to join?
Receptionist:	\$225.00 a year for a single membership, \$270.00 for a family membership.
Harry:	I see . . . Well, I'll have to think about it. Thank you.

SPIN-OFF DIALOGUE

Receptionist: Volner Health Club.

Harry: Hello. Could you tell me something about your health club?

Receptionist: Yes. What do you want to know?

Harry: Do you have a pool and a track for jogging?

Receptionist: Yes, we do. And we also have a weight room if you're interested in weights.

Harry: I used to be, but not any more . . . What's the price of a year's membership?

Receptionist: $225.00 a year for one person and $270.00 for a family.

Harry: Hm . . . Well, I'm going to think it over. Thank you for your help.

USEFUL EXPRESSIONS

Greeting People on the Telephone: *Hello. Volner Health Club* (name of establishment).
Good morning. Volner Health Club.
Good afternoon. Volner Health Club.
Good evening. Volner Health Club.

Expressing Agreement: *Yes.*
Certainly. (formal)
Sure. (informal)

Expressing Approval: *Good.*
(That sounds) *very good.*

Expressing Interest: I'*m interested in* weights.

VOCABULARY

NOUNS
facilities
family
membership
price
receptionist
room
swimming pool
track
weight
year

ADJECTIVE
single

ADVERB
certainly

VERBS
cost
give
jog
join
sound
think about
think over
used to + verb

IDIOMS AND PHRASES
be interested in
I see.
That sounds good.
what kind of

PRACTICE I

1. ***Correct or Incorrect.*** **If the following statements are correct, say, "That's correct." If they are incorrect, say, "That's incorrect." Then make the statements correct.**

examples: It's 9:00 A.M. The receptionist for Sears stores says, "Good morning. Sears and Roebuck." That's correct.

It's 8:00 P.M. The receptionist for Washington College says, "Good afternoon. Washington College." That's incorrect. She/he says, "Good evening. Washington College."

1) You enjoy going to concerts. You're interested in music.
2) When a classmate asks you to explain something, you say, "Sure."
3) At 6:30 P.M. you called up the Palace Theater. The employee who answered the telephone said, "Good afternoon. Palace Theater."
4) Your teacher approves of your pronunciation. He/she says, "Bad!"
5) A family member greets you on the phone. He says, "Hello."
6) Paul has a stamp collection. He's not interested in stamps.
7) A boss asks his/her secretary to type some letters. He/she answers, "Certainly."
8) A friend approves of your suggestion. She says, "That's good."

2. Fill in the blanks with the correct word(s).

example: Good morning. Volner Health Club.

1) Harry isn't interested ____________ weights anymore.
2) At 8:45 P.M. she said on the phone, "Good ____________. Alden's Drugstore."
3) When the telephone rings, you pick up the receiver and say ____________.
4) "Please hold on." The receptionist answered, "____________."
5) That sounds ____________ good.
6) At 3:30 P.M. the receptionist said, "Good ____________. Leo's Restaurant."
7) I know you're ____________ in photography because you're always taking pictures with your camera.
8) At 11:05 A.M. the receptionist said, "Good ____________. Davis Office Machines."

STRUCTURES

A. Infinitives after Nouns or Indefinite Pronouns

It costs **$225.00** *to join* the health club.
I have **nothing** *to do.*
I would like **something** *to do.*

B. More 2–Word Verbs

Separable: *Call up*
Call Mary *up.*
Call up Mary.
Call her *up.*

Other separable 2–word verbs are *look up, pick up, think over,* and *write down.*

PRACTICE II

1. Fill in the blanks with an infinitive from the list.

to read	to eat	to drink
to do	to rest	to learn
to join	to think over	to wear

example: We're thirsty. We want something to drink.

1) She looked in her closet. But she couldn't find anything ____________ to the party.
2) The teacher gave the class ten words ____________ .
3) How much does it cost ____________ that club?
4) I'm very hungry. I want something ____________ .
5) He hasn't made his decision. He has many things ____________ .
6) You were looking for a good book ____________ .
7) They felt bored because they had nothing ____________ .
8) The tired couple tried to find a place ____________ .

2. Make sentences with these cue words.

example: Mary wants to talk to her aunt. (call up)
So she's going to call her up.

1) I can't remember all the new verbs. (write down)
2) The baby doesn't want to walk anymore. (his father) (pick up)
3) We don't have a solution to the problem. (think over)
4) He's on the telephone and he's trying to explain why he was late. But his girlfriend is very angry and won't listen to him. (hang up)
5) You don't understand that word. (look up in your dictionary)
6) Harry might forget the phone number. (write down)
7) I'd like to talk to my friends, but I can't go out. (call up)
8) She doesn't want to call Information for a telephone number. (look up in the telephone book)

TRANSFER

1. You call up the American School. Read the dialogue first; then fill in the blanks with appropriate phrases or sentences. It's 2:30 P.M.

Receptionist: ______________________________.
(Say, "Good afternoon. American School.")

Student: Hello. Could you tell me about your English classes?

Receptionist: ______________________________?
(Say, "Certainly." Ask what he/she would like to know.)

Student: Do you have evening classes for beginners?

Receptionist: ______________________________
(Say, "Yes," and tell him/her that you also have Saturday
______________________________.
morning classes.)

Student: That's good. What's the price of six-week course?

Receptionist: ______________________________.
(Tell him/her the price for six weeks.)

Student: I see. Well, I'm going to think about it. Thank you for your help.

2. You call up the Merton Dance Studio. One of the dance instructors answers the telephone. Read the dialogue first; then fill in the blanks with appropriate phrases or sentences.

Dance Instructor: ______________________________.
(Say, "Merton Dance Studio.")

Student: Hello. Could you give me some information about your dance studio?

Dance Instructor: ________ . ____________________________________ ?
(Say, "Yes." Ask what he/she wants to know.)

Student: What kind of facilities do you have?

Dance Instructor: ____________________________________
(Tell him/her you have a ballroom for group instruction and
____________________________________ .
several small rooms for private lessons.)

Student: I'd like private lessons. How much do they cost?

Dance Instructor: ____________________________________ .
(Tell him/her it's $15.00 an hour for private lessons.)

Student: Thank you. I'm going to think it over.

MAKING A CONVERSATION

Write a conversation with your partner. Choose one of the following situations or try one of your own.

1. You'd like to fly to Mexico, so you call up Mexico Airlines and ask the ticket agent for some information about their flights to Mexico. You want to know if they have a Tuesday morning flight to Mexico City. After the ticket agent tells you that they do, then ask about the price of a one-way ticket.

2. You want to study computer programming, so you call up the admissions office of a local college. You ask the admissions officer if they have an introductory course in computer programming. He/she answers that they have a course in computer basics. Then you ask how much it costs.

Catalogue

TOPICS FOR DISCUSSION

1. What did Harry want to know about the Volner Health Club? Is Harry interested in weights? What sports is he interested in? What sports are you interested in? What sports aren't you interested in?

2. How much does it cost to join the Volner Health Club (for one person, and for a family)?

3. Are you a member of a club? What is it? If you are in America now, did you use to be a member of a club in your country? What was it? How did you join?

UNIT

9

In the Library

Ricky: Excuse me. Is anybody sitting here?

Brenda: Ricky! Hi! No, sit down.

Ricky: Are you doing homework?

Brenda: Yeah. A book report for English class.

Ricky: I have to do a book report, too.

Man: Sssh. Sssh.

Ricky: I'm sorry.

Brenda: Sorry.

Man: That's all right. But if you want to talk, why don't you go outside?

SPIN-OFF DIALOGUE

Ricky: Excuse me. Is this seat taken?

Brenda: Ricky! What a surprise! Sit down.

Ricky: Are you working on a term paper?

Brenda: Yeah. For English class.

Ricky: I've got to do one too, but I haven't thought of a topic yet.

Woman: Sssh.

Ricky: Sorry.

Brenda: Sorry.

Woman: That's all right. But if you're going to talk, please go outside.

USEFUL EXPRESSIONS

Attracting Attention:	*Excuse me . . .*
Expressing Surprise:	*What a surprise!*
Making an Apology:	*I'm sorry.* *Sorry.*
Responding to an Apology:	*That's all right.*
Making a Suggestion:	*Why don't you* go outside?

VOCABULARY

NOUNS	VERBS	IDIOMS AND PHRASES
class	sit	Excuse me.
homework	sit down	I'm sorry.
report	taken (take)	Sorry.
seat	thought (think)	Sssh.
surprise		That's all right.
term paper		
topic		

PRACTICE I

1. Put the words in the correct order to make sentences.

example: a have too report to I do book .
<u>I have to do a book report, too.</u>

1) a what surprise !
2) you go why outside don't ?
3) all right that's .
4) to too got I've do one .

5) sit don't you down why ?
6) me excuse . this taken is seat ?
7) sorry was I talking I'm loudly so .
8) a think to of I topic have .

2. Carry out the following instructions.

example: You step on somebody's foot by accident.
Apologize. Sorry.

1) Attract a woman's attention on the street. Then tell her that she dropped her glove.
2) Everybody is obligated to come to class on time. Express this idea.
3) You see an old friend from your childhood at a party. Express surprise.
4) Your friend lost your magazine. She apologizes. Respond to her apology.
5) A family member can't talk to you now. Suggest that he talk to you later.
6) You didn't study for the test, but you passed. Express surprise.
7) You told your friend's secret. Apologize to her.
8) You are very sick. Say that it is necessary for you to stay in bed.

STRUCTURES

A. Present Tense—Passive Voice

To be (am, is, are) + Past participle
This seat *is* *taken.*

Yes/no Question: *Is* this seat *taken*?

B. Present Perfect Tense with *Already* and *Yet*

have/has	+	past participle
She'*s*	**already**	*thought* of a topic.
or, She'*s*		*thought* of a topic **already.**
He *hasn't*		*thought* of a topic **yet.**

Yes/no Question: *Have* you *thought* of a topic **yet**?

We use the present perfect for an action beginning in the past and continuing up to the present.

We use *already* in positive sentences and *yet* in negative sentences and yes/no questions.

PRACTICE II

1. Choose the correct word to complete the sentences.

example: How is that word **spell/spelling/spelled** ?
How is that word spelled?

1) Are these seats **took/taken/taking** ?
2) Everybody is **done/did/do** .
3) Am I well **think of/thinking of/thought of** ?
4) The desks are **scratching/scratched/scratch** .
5) The glass is **broke/broken/break** .
6) What is that **called/call/calling** ?
7) Are the beds **make/making/made** ?
8) Is your term paper **write/wrote/written** yet?

2. The following checklist shows what Brenda has already done for her term paper and what she hasn't done yet. Make statements with *already* and *yet*.

✓ chosen a topic
✓ bought note cards
✓ done some research
____ read all the necessary books
✓ started taking notes
____ finished taking notes
____ arranged note cards in order
✓ made an outline
____ taken out the unimportant note cards
____ started to write her term paper

examples: She's already done some research.
She hasn't read all the necessary books yet.

TRANSFER

1. You know Brenda very well. You've just gotten on a train and you see an empty seat next to her. Read the dialogue first; then fill in the blanks with appropriate phrases or sentences.

Student: __________. ________________?
(Say, "Excuse me." Ask if this seat is taken.)

Brenda: __________! What a surprise! Sit down.
(your name)

Student: ______________________________?
(Ask Brenda where she is going.)

Brenda: I'm going to Mountainville.

Coincidence Student: Oh! ______________________________.
(Say you're going there too.)

Woman with a baby: Sssh. He just went to sleep.

Student: ______________________________.
(Say that you're sorry.)

Brenda: Sorry.

Woman with a baby: That's all right. Please just talk more quietly.

2. Brenda is watching a beauty contest. You just walked in. There is an empty seat next to Brenda. Read the dialogue first; then fill in the blanks with appropriate phrases or sentences.

Student: ______________________________.
(Say, "Excuse me."

______________________________?
Ask if anybody is sitting here.)

Brenda: __________! Hi! No, sit down.
(your name)

Student: ______________________________?
(Ask if you missed anything.)

Brenda: No, it just started.

Boy: Sssh. Sssh.

Student: ______________________________.
(Say, "Sorry.")

Brenda: Sorry.

Boy: That's all right.

MAKING A CONVERSATION

Write a conversation with your partner. Choose one of the following situations, or try one of your own.

1. You meet a friend unexpectedly in a hospital lounge. There's an empty chair next to him/her. You and your friend begin talking loudly. A sick person who is also in the lounge says "sssh." You apologize and he/she responds to your apology.

2. You are at a meeting at work. A co-worker asks if the seat next to you is taken. You tell him/her "no," and he/she sits down. You continue talking until somebody else asks you to be quiet.

TOPICS FOR DISCUSSION

1. Why did Ricky say "excuse me" to Brenda? What are some other situations when people use this expression? When was the last time you said "excuse me"? Why did you say it?

2. Have you met someone unexpectedly recently? Did you say, "What a surprise!"? Describe the circumstances.

3. Do you think Ricky and Brenda were right to apologize for talking loudly in the library? Why or why not? Can you tolerate a lot of noise? Or do you say "sssh" a lot? Or do you suffer in silence?

4. What are other situations where people say "I'm sorry"? When was the last time you said "I'm sorry"? Did the other person respond to your apology?

5. If someone says "I'm sorry," should you always accept the apology? Why or why not? Can you think of a time when someone said "I'm sorry" to you, but you did not accept the apology? Did you accept it later on?

UNIT 10

Saying Hello to a Friend

Cesar: Hi, Dan.

Dan: Cesar! . . . Do you want to buy something?

Cesar: No. I was in the neighborhood, so I thought I'd come by to say hello.

Dan: Well, it's good to see you. How are you doing?

Cesar: All right. I like my classes and everything.

Dan: That's good.

Cesar: But sometimes I get homesick, and then I . . .

Dan: Look, you'll get over it. It always takes time to get used to a new place.

SPIN-OFF DIALOGUE

Cesar: Hello.

Dan: Cesar! What are you doing here?

Cesar: I was in the area, so I thought I'd drop by to say hello.

Dan: How's everything going?

Cesar: Okay. I like school here a lot.

Dan: That's great.

Cesar: Once in a while I get homesick though, and then I . . .

Dan: Look, it always takes a while to adjust to a new place.

USEFUL EXPRESSIONS

Expressing Result:	I was in the area, *so* I thought I'd come by.
Expressing Certainty:	I *thought* (that) I'd come by. (past) I *think* (that) it's true. (present)
Greetings:	*How are you?* *How are you doing?* (informal) *How's everything going?* (informal)
Expressing Pleasure:	*I like* my classes.
Expressing Intention:	You'*ll* get over it. (you + will)

VOCABULARY

ADJECTIVE
homesick

VERBS
adjust
chat
come by
drop by
get over
get used to
interrupt

IDIOMS AND PHRASES
But I get homesick.
(= I get homesick *though.*)
It takes time.
It takes a while.
once in a while

PRACTICE I

1. Fill in the blanks with the correct word(s).

1) ____________ are you?
2) I ____________ I'd come by.
3) ____________ get over it.
4) She was tired, ____________ she went to bed early.
5) How's everything ____________ ?

6) Some students ____________ they know all the answers.

7) I was in the neighborhood, ____________ I thought I'd drop by.

8) How ____________ you doing?

2. Put the words in the correct order to make sentences.

example: going everything how's ?
<u>How's everything going?</u>

1) it's think that true I .
2) say I'd I by come thought hello to .
3) you how doing are ?
4) it to used you'll get .
5) everything like classes and my I .
6) Dan see wanted Cesar to .
7) went store to so he the .
8) a lot I here like school .

STRUCTURES

A. Adjective + Infinitive

It's *good* **to see** you.

B. Adverbs of Manner and Quantity after Verbs and Direct Objects

Our teacher *speaks* **English *well*.**
We *listen* ***carefully*.**
We *enjoy* our **classes *a lot*.**

We put the adverb of manner or quantity after the verb. When there is a direct object in the sentence we put the adverb of manner or quantity after the direct object. Some irregular adverbs are *fast, hard,* and *well.*

PRACTICE II

1. Make sentences with the cue word(s).

examples: He jogs around the block. (slowly)
He jogs slowly around the block.

I sang the song. (very loudly)
I sang the song very loudly.

1) You worked on your book report. (hard)
2) She answered the question. (correctly)
3) Cesar likes his classes. (very much)
4) I sleep in my own bed. (well)
5) They play the piano. (a little)
6) We talked before the play began. (quietly)
7) Please don't drive in the town. (fast)
8) He said the word. (very softly)

2. Read the following paragraph. Then fill in the blanks with the correct word(s).

Cesar was near Mr. Climo's clothing store, ______ (1) he thought he would drop by ______ (2) hello to his friend. Dan was glad ______ (3) Cesar. Dan asked him ______ (4) he was doing. Cesar replied that he liked ______ (5) a lot, but that ______ (6) he got homesick. Dan told him that it ______ (7) takes a while ______ (8) to a new place.

TRANSFER

1. You are a friend of Dan's from high school. You're working at a gas station now. You meet Dan on the street in front of his home. Read the dialogue carefully; then fill in the blanks with appropriate phrases or sentences.

Student: ______________________________ .
(Say, "Hi Dan.")

Dan: ______________ ! What are you doing here?
(your name)

Student: ______________________________
(Say that you were in the area, so you thought you'd drop by to
______________________________ .
say hello.)

Dan: It's great to see you. How are you doing?

Student: ____________ . ________________________
(Say, "Okay." Tell him you like your job at the gas station.)
____ .

Dan: That's good.

Student: ____
(Tell him but sometimes you miss the good times you and he
____
used to have, and . . .)

Dan: I know what you mean.

2. You know Dan from the beach where you both used to go swimming during your summer vacations. You haven't seen him in a few years. You meet him in the school cafeteria. Read the dialogue carefully; then fill in the blanks with appropriate phrases or sentences.

Student: ____ .
(Say, "Hello.")

Dan: ______________ ! Are you going to school here?
(your name)

Student: __________ . ____________________________ .
(Say, "Yes." Tell him you're a freshman.)

Dan: How have you been?

Student: __________ . ____________________________
(Say, "Fine." Tell him you like your classes and that you've made a
____ .
few friends already.)

Dan: Good.

Student: You know, ______________________________ .
(Tell him you miss Sunrise Beach once in a while.)

Dan: Then why don't you go back there as a lifeguard next summer?

MAKING A CONVERSATION

Write a conversation with your partner. Choose one of the following situations, or try one of your own.

1. You meet an old girlfriend/boyfriend at a museum. You chat. Your old girlfriend/boyfriend tells you that he/she misses the good times you used to have together. You tell him/her that you are married now.

2. You are on a boat at a seaside resort. You meet a friend and chat. Your friend tells you that sometimes he/she gets seasick. Tell your friend that he/she'll get over it if he/she breathes deeply.

TOPICS FOR DISCUSSION

1. Did Cesar go into Mr. Climo's clothing store to buy something? Why did he go in? Do you often visit your friends while they are working?

2. Have you ever gotten homesick? Describe the circumstances. Do you get homesick now? If you do, what do you do to get over it? Or do you feel you can't get over it?

3. Do you think Dan is a sensitive person? Why or why not? Why do you think he interrupted Cesar?

4. How long did it take you to get used to your English class? Are you used to it now? Describe one situation you adjusted to easily. Then describe another situation that was more difficult to adjust to.

PART II

Part II begins one month later in November. Steve, Paula, and Lisa Spock are more settled in now. They have met and gotten to know all their neighbors in the building: Frank and Judy Climo and their sons Dan and Ricky, Carol Wright and her daughter Brenda, and Harry Mullens.

Now it's 8:00 at night. The Spocks are giving a small housewarming, and they have invited their neighbors.

UNIT

11

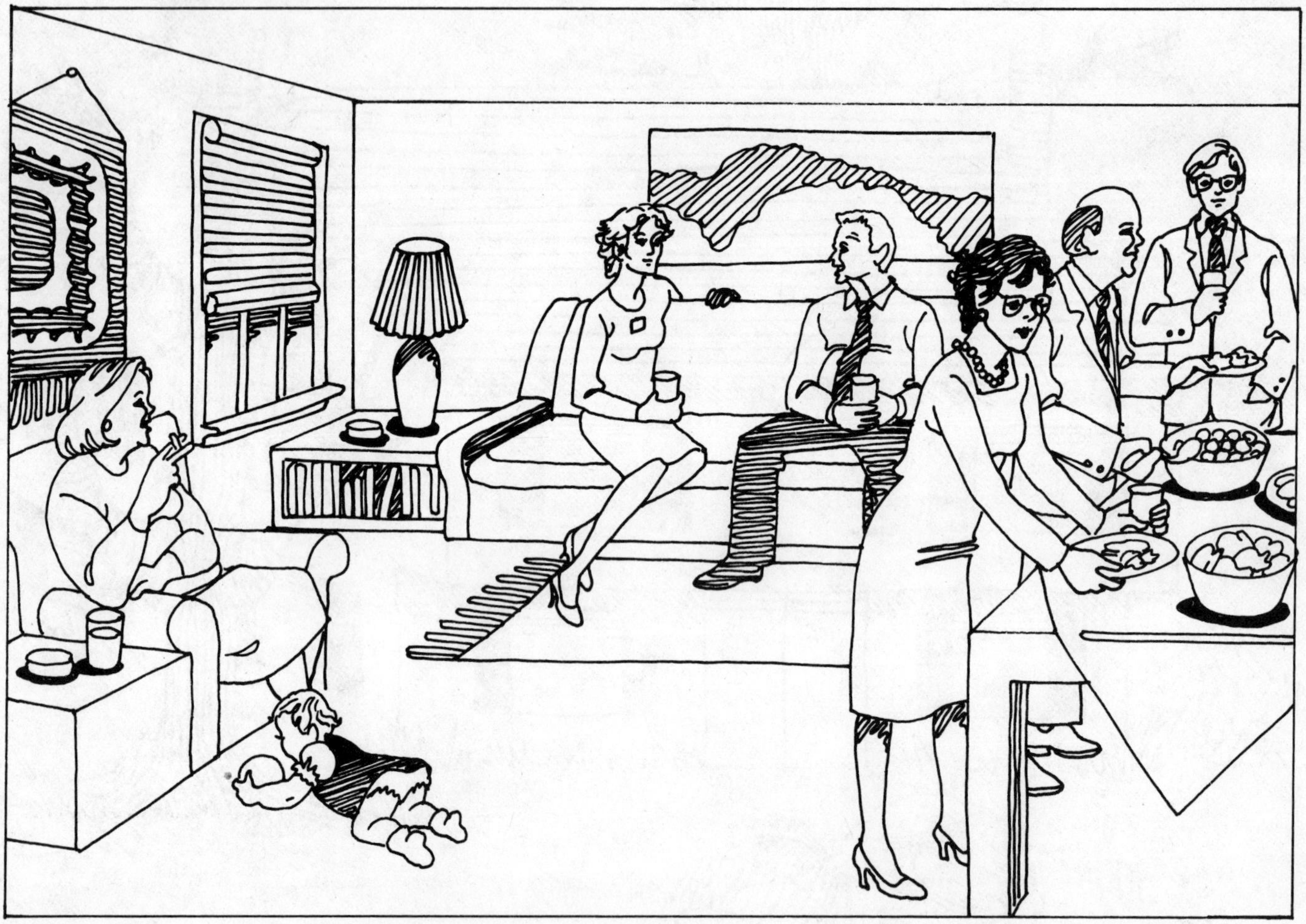

At a Housewarming Party (A)

Making Small Talk

Harry: This is very nice—how you decorated the living room.

Paula: Thank you.

Harry: Where's that from? *(He points to a wall-hanging.)*

Paula: It's from Morocco. My husband and I got it on one of our trips. *(Lisa starts to crawl over to them.)*

Harry: How old is Lisa now?

Paula: Almost a year . . . Oh, I must remember to make an appointment for her—for a checkup with the doctor . . . By the way, did you join that health club?

Harry: No, I didn't. But I *did* join the Y.* It's less expensive and has everything I want.

*YMCA (Young Men's Christian Association). There are Y's in cities and towns all over the U.S.

SPIN-OFF DIALOGUE

Harry: You've decorated your apartment very nicely.

Paula: Thank you.

Harry: What's that over there? *(He points to a wall-hanging.)*

Paula: It's a wall-hanging. Steve and I bought it when we were in Morocco a few years ago. *(Lisa crawls toward them)*

Harry: How old is Lisa?

Paula: She'll be a year next week . . . Oh, I must remember to make an appointment for her year-old checkup . . . By the way, did you join that health club?

Harry: No, I decided not to. I joined the Y instead. It's cheaper.

USEFUL EXPRESSIONS

Expressing Pleasure:	*This is (very)* nice. *It's* nice.
Expressing Obligation/Necessity:	I *must* remember to make an appointment.
Giving a Negative Answer:	*No, I didn't.*
Correcting a Negative Statement:	No, I didn't. But I *did* join the "Y."

VOCABULARY

NOUNS
appointment
checkup
housewarming
necklace
wall-hanging

ADVERBS
almost
less

VERBS
bought (buy)
crawl
decorate
point
remind

IDIOMS AND PHRASES
. . . ago (a few years ago)
by the way
instead
make an appointment
make small talk
on a trip

PRACTICE I

1. Carry out the following instructions.

example: Has Paula called the doctor yet? Give a negative answer.
No, she hasn't.

1) Harry didn't go out yesterday morning. Correct this negative statement, and say that he went out yesterday afternoon.
2) You like your friend's new girlfriend. Express this idea.
3) Say that it is necessary for Paula to make a doctor's appointment for Lisa.

4) Did Harry know where the Spocks' wall-hanging was from? Give a negative answer.

5) Say that you like the spot where you are going to have a picnic.

6) You didn't spend any time with your aunt. Correct this negative statement and say that you also spent some time with your cousin.

7) Is today a holiday? Give a negative answer.

8) Express that you must be home by 5:30.

2. Fill in the blanks with the correct word(s).

example: The baby didn't have any milk.
But she <u>did</u> have some juice.

1) The Spocks liked their new neighbors. They thought they were very ______________ .

2) Did Paula and Steve get their wall-hanging in Egypt? No, ______________ .

3) You ______________ have a driver's license to drive a car.

4) I didn't remember to buy a notebook. But I ______________ remember to buy a pen.

5) Are you wearing a coat? No, ______________ .

6) Her train leaves at 7:20 in the morning. She ______________ get up early.

7) They didn't read the newspaper. But they ______________ watch the news on TV.

8) He liked my new shoes, so he said, "______________ very nice.

STRUCTURES

A. Adjective Comparatives

cheap → cheap*er*
nice → nic*er*

We add *-er* to form the comparative of 1-syllable adjectives. If the 1-syllable adjective ends in silent "e," we just add *-r*.

easy → eas*ier*
fat → fat*ter*

In 2-syllable adjectives ending in "y," we change "y" to "i" and add *-er*.

In 1-syllable adjectives ending in a single final consonant preceded by a single vowel, we double the final consonant, then add *er*.

expensive → more expensive

Gold is *more expensive than* silver.
or, Silver isn't *more expensive than* gold.
or, Silver is *less expensive than* gold.

We use *more* or *less* with adjectives having two or more syllables. *Less* means *not more.* We use *than* when we compare two people or things.

B. Negative Infinitives

He decided *not to join* the health club.

We put *not* before *to* to make a negative infinitive.

Did you join the health club? No, I decided *not to.*

We can omit the verb and its complement (e.g., *join the health club*), when an infinitive phrase is repeated. i.e., in short answers.

PRACTICE II

1. Choose the correct word(s) to complete these sentences.

example: She's **thiner/thinner/more thin** than her brother.
She's thinner than her brother.

1) The "Y" is **cheap/cheaper/more cheaper** than the health club.
2) This department store is **nicer/niceer/more nice** than the one on the corner.
3) It is **more expensive/less expensive/expensiver** to live in New York than in a small town.
4) This room is **big/bigger/biger** than the other one.
5) Your suitcase is **heavyer/heavier/more heavy** than mine.
6) The story of her life is **interestinger/more interesting/more interestinger** than the book I just read.
7) He's **more lazier/lazyer/lazier** than they are.
8) Is the new couch **comfortabler/less comfortabler/less comfortable** than the old one?

2. Make the infinitive phrases in these sentences negative.

example: We promised to stay out late.
We promised not to stay out late.

1) I'll try to worry.
2) She decided to take along her son.

3) Harry preferred to join a health club.
4) The children promised to leave the house.
5) You must try to listen to him.
6) We decided to bring our lunch.
7) They prefer to ask their teacher for help.
8) He promised to forget his doctor's appointment.

TRANSFER

1. You are having a meal with Paula at a nice restaurant. You compliment her on her necklace. Read the dialogue first; then fill in the blanks with appropriate phrases or sentences.

Student: ____.
(Tell Paula her necklace is very nice.)

Paula: Thank you.

Student: ____?
(Ask where she got it.)

Paula: At the little jewelry store on Third Street. You know, the one next to the bakery.

(The waiter brings your food.)

Student: ____.
(Tell Paula the waiter looks a little like her brother.

____?
Ask her how old he is now.)

Paula: He's twenty . . . That reminds me, I must remember to write him . . . By the way, did you see *your* brother last week?

Student: ____.
(Tell her that you didn't.

____.
But you did speak to him on the phone.)

2. Harry is visiting you in your new office. Read the dialogue first; then fill in the blanks with appropriate phrases or sentences.

Harry: Your office is very nice.

Student: ____.
(Say "Thank you.")

Harry: Where did you get that from? *(He points to a shell.)*

Student: ____
(Tell him you got it in Florida when you were there last winter.)

____.

(Harry looks at a photograph of a child on your desk.)

Harry: How old is ____________ now?
(name)

Student: ____
(Tell Harry he/she's going to be seven next week and that

____.

you must remember to buy him/her a birthday present.

____

Ask Harry if by the way he bought Robert anything for his birthday.)

____?

Harry: No, I didn't. But I *did* send him a card.

MAKING A CONVERSATION

Write a conversation with your partner. Choose one of the following situations, or try one of your own.

1. A friend visits you, and you go to a nearby park. He likes it. He asks you what is on the other side of the park. You tell him it's a zoo. A couple with a little girl walk by. Your friend asks you how old your niece is now. You answer and then say that you must remember to tell her mother something. Finally you ask your friend something, beginning with "by the way."

2. A member of your family visits you. He/she is wearing a new jacket. Compliment him/her on it. Then ask him/her where he/she bought it. Ask the member of your family if he/she knows when the birthday of another relative is. He/she answers and then tells you he/she must remember to get something for your relative. Then he/she asks you something, beginning with "by the way."

TOPICS FOR DISCUSSION

1. Does Harry Mullens like the way the Spocks decorated their living room? How do you know? Do you like the way your living room is decorated? Why or why not?

2. Where is the wall-hanging from? When did Steve and Paula Spock buy it? Do you have anything from other countries in your living room? If you do, what are they? Where are they from?

3. One makes appointments with professionals, e.g., lawyers, doctors, or teachers, or for business purposes. Did you make any appointments this week? If you did, who were they with? Do you have to remember to make any other appointments soon? If you do, who are they with?

4. Harry didn't join the health club but he *did* join the YMCA. Have you changed your mind about anything lately?

UNIT
12

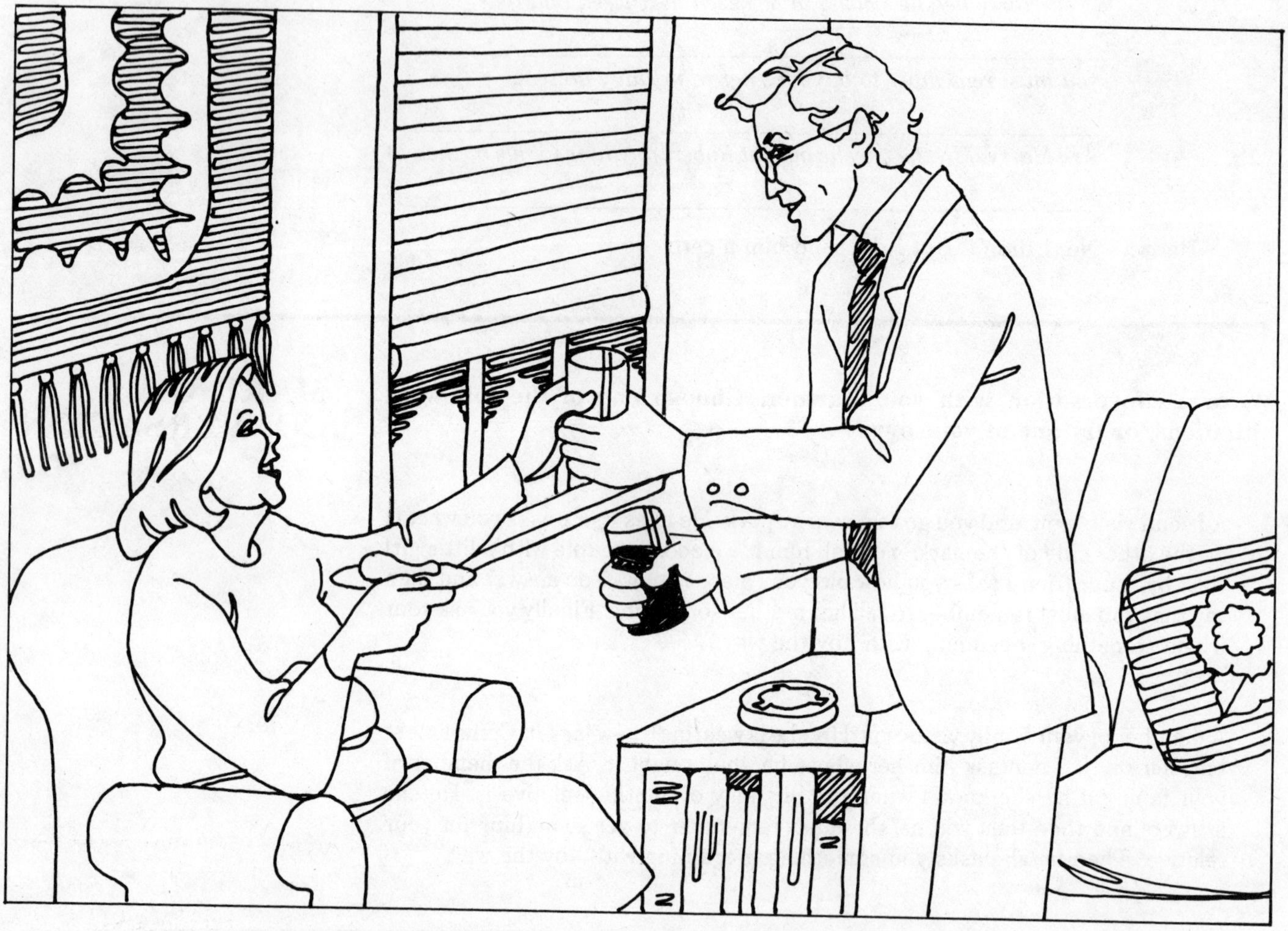

At a Housewarming Party (B)

Eating Too Much

Carol: I can't stop eating this chicken. It's delicious.

Steve: Thank you. It's one of Paula's specialties. Have you tried the potato salad?

Carol: No. I don't like potato salad. But I had some fruit salad and three pieces of the homemade bread.

Steve: Can I get you something more to drink?

Carol: Yes, please. *(She gives him her glass.)*

Steve: The same as this?

Carol: Yes. *(to herself)* I should go on a diet . . . But not tonight. I'll start it tomorrow.

SPIN-OFF DIALOGUE

Carol: I can't stop eating these meatballs. They're so good.

Steve: I know. They're one of Paula's favorite dishes too. Have you tried the baked beans?

Carol: No, I haven't. I don't like beans. But I had some tossed salad and a few pieces of the homemade bread.

Steve: Can I get you some more wine?

Carol: Yes, please. *(She hands him her glass.)*

Steve: The same kind?

Carol: Yes. *(to herself)* I should really go on a diet. But I can't start it now . . . Maybe tomorrow.

USEFUL EXPRESSIONS

Expressing Inability:	I *can't* start it now.
Expressing Displeasure:	I *don't like* potato salad.
Making an Offer:	*Can I* get you some more wine? (verb)
Accepting an Offer or Invitation:	*Yes, please.* *Thank you.*

VOCABULARY

NOUNS
album
ashtray
baked beans
chicken
dish
kind
meatballs
party
piece
potato
specialty
tossed salad
wine

ADJECTIVES
delicious
fabulous
favorite
homemade
same
tossed

VERBS
avoid
consider
hand
quit
regret
start

IDIOMS AND PHRASES
go on a diet

PRACTICE I

1. Fill in the blanks with the correct word(s).

example: He never wears anything yellow because he doesn't like that color.

1) Carol ____________ stop eating the meatballs.
2) She didn't eat any baked beans because she ____________ like them.
3) Can I ____________ you something to drink?
4) Yes, ____________. I'd like a cup of tea.
5) I can't ____________ my diet now.
6) You ____________ like Ted, but he likes you.
7) ____________ I help you with your homework?
8) ____________ you.

2. *Correct or Incorrect.* If the following statements are correct, say, "That's correct." If they are incorrect, say, "That's incorrect." Then make them correct.

examples: You offer to pay for your friend's ticket.
You say, "Can I pay for your ticket?"
That's correct.

Your friend accepts your offer and says,
"No, thank you."
That's incorrect. He/she says, "Thank you."

1) The little baby isn't able to crawl yet. He can't crawl yet.
2) The TV program isn't very good. You express your displeasure and say, "I don't like the program."
3) Your friend offers you some fruit. You accept and say, "Yes, please."
4) You express your dislike of very cold weather and say, "I like very cold weather."
5) You aren't able to learn the new song by tomorrow. You say, "I can learn the new song by tomorrow."
6) You offer to get your friend a magazine. You say, "Can you get me a magazine?"
7) Your friend accepts your offer and says, "Thank you."
8) They aren't able to ride a bicycle. They can ride a bicycle.

STRUCTURES

A. *A little* and *A few*

With mass nouns use *a little*:	*a little* information *a little* ice cream *a little* money
With count nouns use *a few*:	*a few* pages *a few* cookies *a few* dollars

B. Units of Measure with Mass Nouns

Singular:	*a piece* of bread *a glass* of water *a can* of oil	Plural:	(three) *pieces* of bread (a few) *glasses* of water (some) *cans* of oil

C. Verb + Gerund

We *stopped* **eating.**
You *finished* **telling** the joke.
I *suggested* **going** home.

Other verbs that take gerunds include: *avoid, consider,* and *regret.*

PRACTICE II

1. Choose the correct words to complete these sentences.

examples: She asked for **a little/a few** advice.
She asked for a little advice.

They wrote down **a little/a few** questions.
They wrote down a few questions.

1) Steve ate **a little/a few** salad.
2) I only have **a little/a few** gold jewelry.
3) She put **a little/a few** crackers on her plate.
4) You invited **a little/a few** friends to come to your apartment.
5) They got **a little/a few** information about the new machine.
6) Do you want **a little/a few** help?
7) He visited them **a little/a few** days ago.
8) There are **a little/a few** chairs in our room.

2. Make sentences with the cue words and numbers.

example: I bought some soup. (four) (can)
I bought four cans of soup.

1) He drank some milk. (two) (glass)
2) You moved some furniture. (five) (piece)
3) Carol ate some homemade bread. (three) (slice)
4) They would like some coffee. (four) (cup)
5) There's some sugar on the shelf. (three) (box)
6) We had some cereal. (two) (bowl)
7) She decided to buy some potatoes. (three) (pound)
8) Did you get any vegetable oil? (two) (bottle)

3. Answer these questions.

example: Where did she suggest going?
She suggested going to the movies.

1) What does he avoid doing?
2) Where did they stop going after school?
3) What did you regret doing?
4) What did she finish doing before she went to the party?
5) What did they avoid doing late at night?
6) What can't Carol stop doing?
7) What language will you and your friend consider studying after English?
8) What did Ed suggest doing?

TRANSFER

1. You are a weekend guest of the Spocks. They have let you play their stereo. Read the dialogue first; then fill in the blanks with appropriate phrases or sentences.

Student: ______________________________.
(Tell Steve you can't stop playing this record.
______________________________.
It's fabulous.)

Steve: Thank you. It's one of my favorites too.
Have you played any of our classical albums?

Student: __________. ______________________________
(Say, "No." Tell him you don't like classical music, but you've already

____ .

listened to two of his jazz records.)

Steve: Can I empty your ashtray?

Student: ____ .

(You give him the ashtray.)

Steve: Do you have enough cigarettes?

Student: ____________ . ____________________________________ .

(Say, "Yes." Tell him you have another pack in your suitcase.)

____

(to yourself) (Say you should really quit smoking, but not 'til you finish the

____ .

other pack.)

2. You are reading a book that Steve gave you. Read the dialogue first; then fill in the blanks with appropriate phrases or sentences.

Student: ____

(Tell Steve that this mystery is terrific, and that you can't put it down.)

____ .

Steve: I know. I couldn't stop reading it either. Have you read anything by Lillian Stockser?

Student: ____ .

(Say, "No," but you read The Last Witness *by Paul Blackburn.)*

Steve: Can I give you another mystery by Blackburn? I don't want it anymore.

Student: ____ .

(Say, "Okay, thank you.")

____

(to yourself) (Say you should stop reading all these mysteries

____ .

and study for your exams.)

MAKING A CONVERSATION

Write a conversation with your partner. Choose one of the following situations, or try one of your own.

1. A family member, who is a photographer, gave you a camera. You can't stop taking pictures. He/she asks you if you've taken any pictures of the old buildings in your neighborhood. Later on he/she offers to give you another roll of color film. Accept his/her offer.

2. You are at a friend's house. He/she gave you a delicious drink. You can't stop drinking it. There's also some ice cream and cake on the table. He/she asks you if you've tried the ice cream. Tell him/her you don't like strawberry ice cream,

but that you had a little piece of cake. Your friend offers to get you a napkin. Accept his/her offer.

TOPICS FOR DISCUSSION

1. What can't Carol Wright stop doing? Why? Is there some food you can't stop eating? If there is, what is it?

2. Has Carol tried Paula's potato salad? Why not? What else did she have? Of all the different kinds of food at the party, which do you like? Which don't you like? What kinds of food do you prepare for parties?

3. What does Steve offer to get Carol? Does she accept his offer? Is Steve a good host? Why do you think so? What are the responsibilities of a good host?

4. Does Carol think she should eat so much? What should she do? Can she start it now? Should you change anything about yourself, e.g., go on a diet or quit smoking? Can you do it now?

5. Do you think Carol will start her diet tomorrow? Why or why not? Why is it so hard to change?

UNIT

13

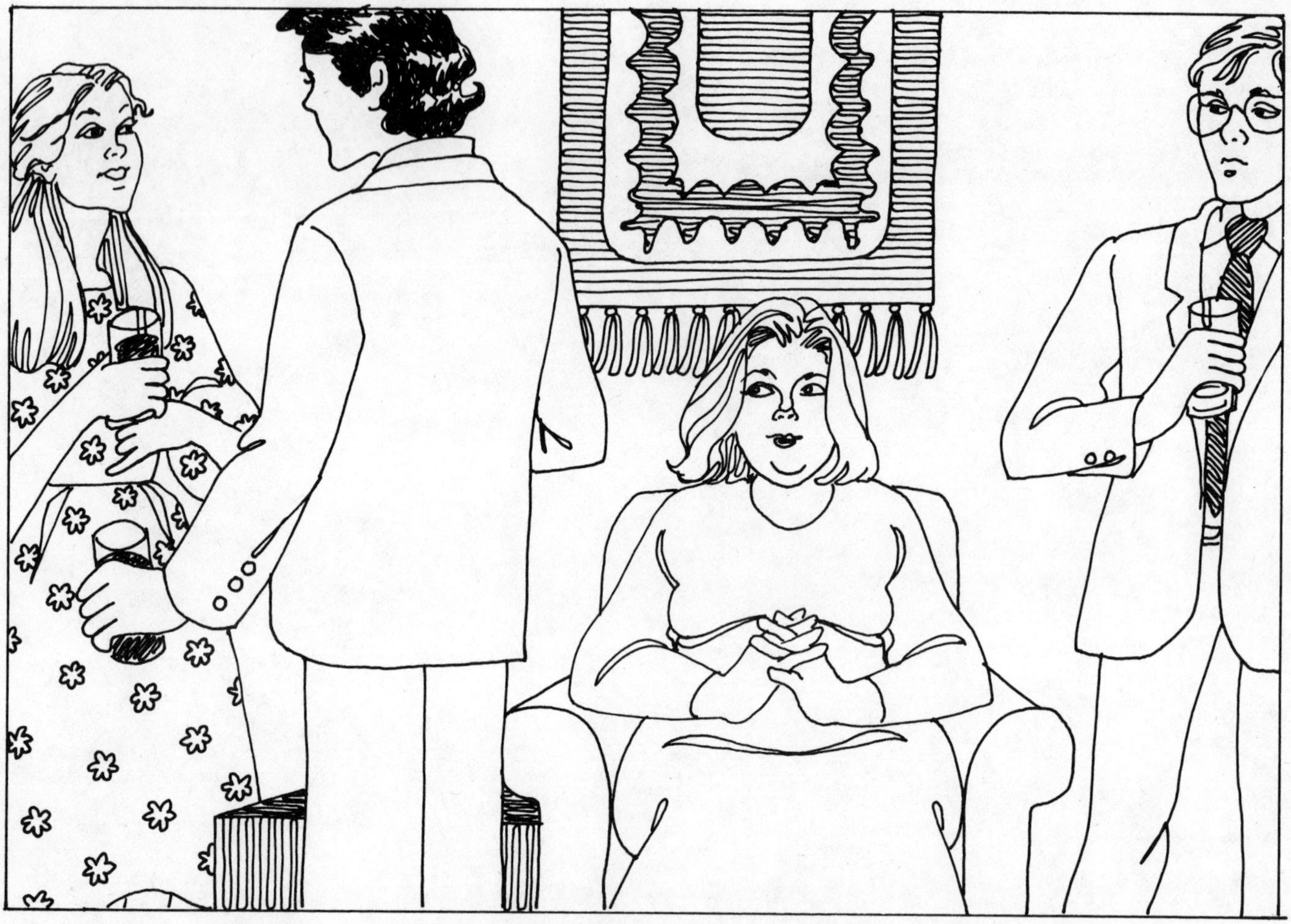

At a Housewarming Party (C)

Making a Date

Dan: You're looking very pretty tonight. Is that a new dress?

Brenda: Yes, it is.

Dan: You've really grown up . . . Say, Brenda, are you doing anything Friday night?

Brenda: No, I don't think so.

Dan: Do you want to go out?

Brenda: Uh. . . I don't know. I've never gone out with anyone in college before . . . I'll have to ask my mother. *(to her mother)* Mom, Dan wants me to go out with him. Can I go?

Mrs. Wright: Yes, I guess it's okay. Just be careful.

SPIN-OFF DIALOGUE

Dan: You're looking very attractive tonight. Are those new earrings?

Brenda: Yes, they are.

Dan: Say, Brenda, do you have plans for Friday night?

Brenda: No, I don't.

Dan: Would you like to go out someplace together?

Brenda: Uh... I don't know... I think I should ask my mother. *(to her mother)* Mother, Dan wants to go out with me. Can I go?

Mrs. Wright: Dan? . . . I guess it's all right. Yes, you can.

USEFUL EXPRESSIONS

Expressing Certainty and Uncertainty: I *think* (that) I should ask my mother.
I don't think so. (negative)

Inviting Others: *Would you like to* go out?

Seeking Permission: *Can I go?* (informal)
May I go? (formal)

Giving Permission: *Yes, you can.* (informal)
Yes, you may. (formal)

VOCABULARY

NOUNS
college
date
earrings
parade
plan
spouse

ADJECTIVES
attractive
pretty

VERBS
grown up (grow up)

IDIOMS AND PHRASES
distant relative
go out (with someone)
I don't think so.
make a date

PRACTICE I

1. **Put the words in the correct order to make sentences.**

example: so I think don't .
<u>I don't think so.</u>

1) with can out Dan I go ?
2) can you yes .
3) think they so don't .
4) together to out would go you someplace like ?
5) I him go with out may ?

6) may yes you .
7) doesn't so Brenda think .
8) go like there you would to ?

2. Carry out the following instructions.

example: Seek permission at a large company to use the bathroom.
<u>May I use the bathroom</u>?

1) Is today a good day to go swimming? Say that you are not certain.
2) You are a teacher. Grant permission to a student to leave the room.
3) Invite somebody to go out for dinner.
4) Have you already made plans for tomorrow night? Say that you are not certain.
5) You are at a distant relative's house. Seek permission to have a glass of water.
6) Are you going to relax now? Express that you are not certain.
7) Seek permission from a friend to drop by at nine o'clock.
8) Give permission to your friend in (7).

STRUCTURES

A. Verb + Infinitive

Subject +	*Verb* +	*Object* +	*Infinitive (Phrase)*
He	invited	her	to go out with him.
Mrs. Wright	allowed	Brenda	to go out with him.

After some verbs we must use an object before the infinitive. We understand the object as the subject of the action that is expressed by the infinitive. Among these verbs are *allow, invite, teach,* and *tell.*

Subject +	*Verb* +	*Object* +	*Infinitive (Phrase)*
He	wanted		to go out.
He	wanted	her	to go out with him.

After certain other verbs there may or may not be an object before the infinitive. Among this group of verbs are *want, prefer,* and *ask.*

B. Adverbs of Frequency

It *always* **takes** time to adjust.
They'**re** *often* busy.

We put the adverb of frequency before the main verb, except for *to be.* We put the adverb of frequency after the verb *to be.* Some adverbs of frequency are *always, often, sometimes, usually, rarely,* and *never.* Some adverbs of frequency may also appear first or last in a sentence.

PRACTICE II

1. Fill in the blanks with the correct form of the verb in parentheses.

The Spocks invited all their neighbors to come (1) (come) to their housewarming party. Mrs. Wright allowed her daughter ________ (2) (wear) a little makeup. At the party Dan asked Brenda ________ (3) (go out) on a date. He wanted her ________ (4) (say) "yes." Brenda asked her mother's permission. Mrs. Wright said that Brenda could go out with Dan. But she told her daughter ________ (5) (be) careful. Mrs. Wright didn't have to say this because she has already taught Brenda ________ (6) (look out) for herself.

2. Answer these questions with the cue words.

example: How often have they taken the train? (rarely)
They've rarely taken the train.

1) How often will he teach the class? (usually)
2) How often have you felt like that? (I) (sometimes)
3) How often has it rained this month? (rarely)
4) How often can you help us out? (we) (always)
5) How often have we interrupted you? (never)
6) How often must I check my work? (always)
7) How often has she missed a meeting? (never)
8) How often should I take his advice? (sometimes)

TRANSFER

1. You are standing on a street corner with your husband/wife/boyfriend/girlfriend/friend. Dan comes by on his motorcycle and says hello. Read the dialogue first; then fill in the blanks with appropriate phrases or sentences.

Dan: Are you doing anything special right now?

Student: ________________________________.
(Say, "No," you aren't.)

Dan: Would you like a ride on my motorcycle?

Student: ______________________________________

(Say, "Yes," but you think you should ask __________ *(name)*

______________________________________.

if it's all right with him/her. Then ask if it's okay with him/

______________________________________?

her if you go with Dan for a short ride on his motorcycle.)

Other Person: Yes. Just be careful.

2. You see Brenda at a parade. She's with her mother who's sitting down and isn't interested in the parade. Read the dialogue first; then fill in the blanks with appropriate phrases or sentences.

Student: ______________________________________?

(Ask Brenda if she can see anything.)

Brenda: No, I can't.

Student: ______________________________________

(Ask her if she wants to go over there with you where you

______________________________________?

can see better.)

Brenda: Yes. Let me just ask my mother.

(to her mother) __________ *(your name)* wants me to go over there—where there's a better view. Can I go with him/her?

Mrs. Wright: Yes, you can.

MAKING A CONVERSATION

Write a conversation with your partner. Choose one of the following situations, or try one of your own.

1. You are at a formal dance. You see a pretty girl or woman. She is sitting next to a man. You ask her to dance. She asks her companion's permission. He gives it to her.

2. You are traveling with your spouse or a friend in a foreign country. You meet a local resident. He/she invites you to go to an interesting place nearby. Your spouse/friend doesn't feel like walking anymore and wants to go back to the hotel. You ask your spouse/friend's permission to go with the local resident. He/she gives you permission.

TOPICS FOR DISCUSSION

1. Did Dan give Brenda a compliment? What was it? Did somebody give you a compliment today? If so, what was it? What was the last compliment you received or gave?

2. Is Brenda doing anything Friday night? Are you doing anything Friday night? If you are, what is it? Do you have plans for tomorrow afternoon? If you do, what are they?

3. Does Brenda want to go out with Dan? Why doesn't she know? Whose permission does she think she should ask? Does her mother give her permission? Do you think Mrs. Wright trusts Brenda? Why?

4. Do you think a fifteen-year-old girl should go out with an eighteen-year-old college boy? Why or why not? When you were fifteen, did you go out on dates? If you did, where did you go?

UNIT
14

Borrowing Some Sugar

Cesar: *(There is a knock at the door.)* Coming . . . Who is it?

Tom: Tom. *(Cesar opens the door.)* I'm sorry to bother you. But do you have any sugar I could borrow? I just ran out.

Cesar: Sure. Come in. *(He gives him some sugar.)* Here.

Tom: Thank you.

Cesar: You're welcome . . . I was just getting myself a cup of coffee. Do you want some too?

Tom: Yes, that would be nice . . . You're from South America, aren't you?

Cesar: Yes, I am . . . From Peru.

SPIN-OFF DIALOGUE

Cesar: *(The doorbell rings.)* Who is it?

Tom: It's me. Tom. *(Cesar opens the door.)* Sorry to bother you. But I just ran out of milk. Could you lend me some?

Cesar: Yeah. No problem . . . Come in. *(He gives him some milk.)* Here you are.

Tom: Thanks.

Cesar: You're welcome . . . I was just making myself some tea. Do you want a cup too?

Tom: Yes, that'd be nice . . . You come from somewhere in Latin America, don't you?

Cesar: Yes. I come from Peru.

USEFUL EXPRESSIONS

Expressing Agreement:	*Sure.* (informal) *Certainly.* (formal)
When Handing Someone Something:	*Here.* *Here you are.*
Responding to Gratitude:	*You're welcome.*
Asking for Information (Tag Question):	You're from South America, *aren't you?*
Giving an Affirmative Answer:	*Yes, I am.*

VOCABULARY

NOUNS
doorbell
problem
role
seasickness
somewhere
sugar

PRONOUN
myself

VERBS
borrow
bother
come in
knock
lend
ran out of (run)
ring

IDIOMS AND PHRASES
come from
make + (food or drink)
No problem.
Yeah.

ADJECTIVES
welcome

PRACTICE I

1. Carry out the following instructions.

example: Ask with a tag question if he borrowed some sugar.
He borrowed some sugar, didn't he?

1) Your classmate thanks you for explaining a difficult word to her. Respond to her expression of gratitude.

2) Did you get up on time this morning? Answer affirmatively.

3) Say something as you hand your friend his sweater.
4) With a tag question, ask another person if you've met someplace before.
5) "Is it okay if I sit here?" Express agreement informally.
6) Ask with a tag question if they were working.
7) Can you cook well? Answer affirmatively.
8) You bought a shirt. The salesperson hands it to you in a bag. What does he/she say to you?

2. Fill in the blanks with the correct word(s).

example: Thanks for giving me a hand. You're welcome.

1) They come from California, ______________?
2) When Cesar gave Tom the sugar, he said, "______________ you are."
3) Were you sleeping when I rang the doorbell? Yes, ______________.
4) You're going to lend them your notes, ______________?
5) Thank you for calling back. ______________ welcome.
6) Is Anne bothering you? Yes, ______________.
7) When the teacher handed the students some paper, she said, "______________."
8) Could you spell that again? ______________.

STRUCTURES

A. Inseparable 2- and 3-Word Verbs

Tom *ran out of* **sugar**.	Tom *ran out of* **it**.
She'*s getting over* **her cold**.	She'*s getting over* **it**.
We'*ll go over* **our notes**.	We'*ll go over* **them**.
I'*ve looked into* **the problems**.	I'*ve looked into* **them**.

We put the noun or pronoun direct object after the inseparable 2- or 3-word verb.

B. Present Modal—WOULD without Understood Condition (*If*-Clause)

Would Be	+	Adjective
That *would be* (That'*d*)		**nice.**

We use *would* for the present time when the condition (*if*-clause) is understood.

C. Present Modal—WOULD (with Improbable Condition) (Infinitive plus Phrase)

Would Be	+ Adjective	+ Infinitive plus Phrase
It *would be* (It'*d*)	**hard**	***to learn three languages at the same time.***

We also use *would* for the present time when the condition (infinitive plus phrase) is very improbable.

PRACTICE II

1. Change the pronoun direct objects to noun direct objects.

example: You got over it.
You got over your illness.

1) We're going to run out of them very soon.
2) Did you look into it carefully?
3) Go over them to look for mistakes.
4) Ken tried to get over it.
5) I must look into them.
6) She ran out of it last night.
7) Have you gotten over it yet?

2. Make sentences with these cue words, using *would*.

Examples: (it) (be interesting) (get to know her)
It would be interesting to get to know her.
or, It'd be interesting to get to know her.

1) (we) (be happy) (take you with us)
2) (you) (be crazy) (believe him)
3) (it) (be difficult) (move to New York without a job)
4) (that) (be very expensive)
5) (it) (be nice) (see them again)
6) (it) (be boring) (do it every day)
7) (she) (be wonderful) (in that role in the play)
8) (it) (be terrible) (have a car accident)

TRANSFER

1. **You ring Cesar's doorbell because you want to borrow a stamp. Read the dialogue first; then fill in the blanks with appropriate phrases or sentences.**

Cesar: Coming . . . Who is it?

Student: ______________ . *(Cesar opens the door.)*
(your name)

______________________________ .
(Say you're sorry to bother him.

______________________________ ?
Ask if he has a stamp you could borrow.)

Cesar: Sure. Come in. *(He gives you a stamp.)* Here you are.

Student: ______________________________ .

Cesar: You're welcome. I was just getting myself a bowl of soup. Do you want some too?

Student: ______________________________ .
(Give an affirmative answer. Ask if he comes from South America.)

______________________________ ?

Cesar: Yes, I do. From Peru.

2. **Tom knocks on your door because he wants to borrow a pen. Read the dialogue first; then fill in the blanks with appropriate phrases or sentences.**

Student: ______________ . ______________________ ?
(Say, "Coming." Ask who it is.)

Tom: Tom. *(You open the door.)* Sorry to bother you. But could you lend me a pen? Mine just ran out of ink.

Student: __________ . __________ . __________ .
(Say, "Yeah. No problem. Come in.") (You give Tom a pen.)

______________________________ .
(Tell him this one works very well.)

Tom: Thank you.

Student: ______________________________

______________________________ .

Tom: That would be very nice . . . You're from ______________ ?
(country where you're from)

Student: ______________________________ .
(Give an affirmative answer.)

MAKING A CONVERSATION

Write a conversation with your partner. Choose one of the following situations, or try one of your own.

1. A neighbor knocks on your door because she just ran out of butter. She wants you to lend her some. You give her a stick of butter. She thanks you, and you respond to her expression of gratitude. Then you ask her if she wants a glass of soda. She accepts your offer and with a tag question asks you if you've lived in this city a long time. Answer with a positive short answer.

2. A friend rings your doorbell because he needs to borrow your typewriter. You lend him your typewriter. He thanks you, and you respond to his expression of gratitude. Then you ask him if he has time for a cup of coffee. He answers with a positive short answer.

TOPICS FOR DISCUSSION

1. Who knocked on Tom's door? Did anybody knock on your door or ring the doorbell yesterday? If somebody did, what did he/she want?

2. Was Tom sorry to bother Cesar? What did he want to borrow? Why? When was the last time you said, "Sorry to bother you, but . . ."? Describe the circumstances.

3. Did Cesar lend Tom any sugar? Have you lent anybody anything recently? What did they borrow from you? What have you borrowed recently? In *Hamlet* by Shakespeare, Polonius says "Neither a borrower, nor a lender be." Is this good advice? Why? Do you follow it? Why or why not?

4. What country does Cesar come from? What country are you from? The continents are North America, South America, Europe, Asia, Africa, Australia, and Antarctica. What continent does Cesar come from? What continent are you in now? What continent do you come from?

UNIT

15

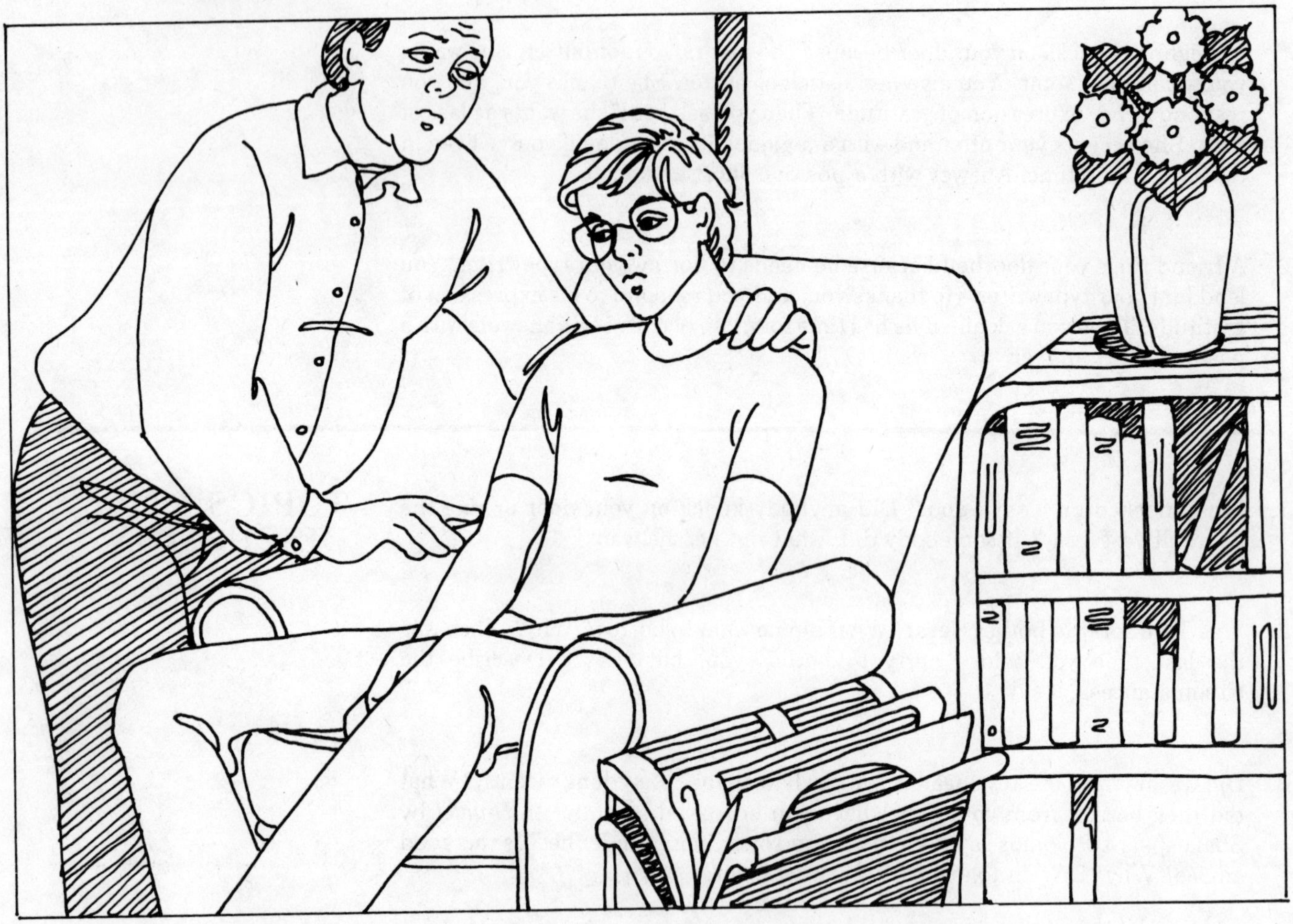

A Father and Son Chat

Mr. Climo: What's the matter, Ricky?

Ricky: Nothing.

Mr. Climo: What is it, son?

Ricky: Did you see Dan ask Brenda out?

Mr. Climo: No. But why shouldn't he ask her out if he wants?

Ricky: Yeah, why not? It's a free country. I don't care.

Mr. Climo: You *do* care. Why don't you ask her out yourself another time?

Ricky: No, I can't now.

SPIN-OFF DIALOGUE

Mr. Climo: What's wrong, Ricky?

Ricky: Nothing.

Mr. Climo: You can tell me, son.

Ricky: Did you know that Dan made a date with Brenda?

Mr. Climo: No. But why shouldn't he if he wants to?

Ricky: That's right. Why not? It doesn't matter at all.

Mr. Climo: But it *does* matter to you. Why don't you ask her out too?

Ricky: Oh, come on, Dad. She'll never go out with me. Not after Dan.

USEFUL EXPRESSIONS

Inquiring about One's Well-being: *What's the matter?*
What's wrong?

Expressing Agreement: *Right.*
That's right.

Expressing Indifference: *I don't care.*
It doesn't matter.

Correcting a Negative Statement: (Speaker A) I don't care.
(Speaker B) You *do* care.

VOCABULARY

NOUNS
Dad
matter
sidelines

ADJECTIVES
free
right
wrong

VERBS
admit
ask out
care
go out
matter

IDIOMS AND PHRASES
at all
Come on.
It's a free country.

PRACTICE I

1. **Put these words in the correct order to make sentences.**

example: care he doesn't .
He doesn't care.

1) matter Ricky the what's , ?
2) right that's . not why ?
3) to but matter it you *does* .

4) I care don't . *do* care you .

5) Ricky , wrong what's ?

6) with that he brother a Brenda his made does care date ?

7) country free a it's . right that's .

8) at it all matter doesn't .

2. *Correct or Incorrect.* If the following statements are correct, say, "That's correct." If they are incorrect, say, "That's incorrect." Then make the statements correct.

example: You just got sick and can't go to the movies. You express indifference and say, "I don't care." That's correct.

Your companion disagrees with you and says, "You care." That's incorrect. He/she says, "You *do* care."

1) The student next to you is crying. You inquire about his emotional state and say, "Is this a free country?"

2) You forgot to bring your dictionary today. You express indifference and say, "It doesn't matter."

3) Why shouldn't they go out together? You express agreement and say, "That's wrong."

4) You said, "I don't know that man." Your friend corrects you and says, "You *do* know him."

5) A family member lost the puzzle she borrowed from you. You express indifference and say, "I care."

6) A girl is sitting on the stairs outside your apartment building. She's trying to stand up, but she can't. You inquire about her well-being and say, "What is it?"

7) You said, "I didn't have a date last night." Your friend disagrees with you and says, "But you *did* see your boyfriend after school."

8) Ricky chatted with his father, didn't he? You express agreement and say, "Right."

STRUCTURES

A. Verbs of Perception—*See, Hear,* etc.

	Sense Verb	+	*Agent*	+	*Verb (Base Form)*
Did you	see / hear		Dan / him		ask her out?

After verbs of perception use the base form of the verb which follows the agent of the completed action. Other verbs of sense perception that take agents plus the base form of verbs include *feel, notice* and *watch.*

B. Reflexive Pronouns

myself	ourselves
yourself	yourselves
himself, herself, itself	themselves

Why don't you ask her out yourself?

(subject) (emphatic reflexive)

We use reflexive pronouns to emphasize the subject of the sentence. The reflexive pronoun usually appears at the end of the sentence.

PRACTICE II

1. Make sentences with the cue words.

example: She followed that woman. (I saw)
I saw her follow that woman.

1) He yelled at me. (you heard)
2) They came in. (did you see)
3) The water got colder in the bathtub. (she felt)
4) We played tennis. (did you watch)
5) The doorbell rang. (did they hear)
6) The bus drove away. (I noticed)
7) The school children crossed the street. (he watched)
8) I closed the door. (you saw)

2. Fill in the blanks with the correct word.

example: He did everything himself.

1) We usually make breakfast ______________ .
2) Did you finish everything ______________ ? (plural)
3) She corrected her mistake ______________ .
4) You don't have to help me. I can do it ______________ .
5) They took down the pictures ______________ .
6) Will he ask her out ______________ ?
7) We can hang up the curtains ______________ .
8) Why don't you apologize to them ______________ ? (singular)

TRANSFER

1. Mr. Climo sees you sitting alone. Something is bothering you. Read the dialogue first; then fill in the blanks with the appropriate words or phrases.

Mr. Climo: What's the matter, ______________________________?
(student's name)

Student: ______________________________.
(Say, "Nothing.")

Mr. Climo: What is it?

Student: ______________________________
(Ask if he saw Nancy give David a ride in her car.)
______________________________?

Mr. Climo: No. But why shouldn't she give him a ride if she wants?

Student: ______________________________.
(Agree with him.
______________________________.
Tell him that you don't really care anyway.)

Mr. Climo: You *do* care. Why don't you ask her why she did it?

Student: ______________________________.

2. Ricky is sitting on the sidelines. He isn't playing soccer with his team today. Read the dialogue first; then fill in the blanks with appropriate phrases or sentences.

Student: ______________________________?
(Ask what's wrong.)

Ricky: Nothing.

Student: ______________________________.

Ricky: Did you hear the coach say I couldn't play in the game?

Student: ______________ . ______________?
(Say you didn't. Ask him why the coach shouldn't make that decision.)

Ricky: That's right. It doesn't matter.

Student: ______________________________ . ______________
(Say that he does care about playing. Suggest that Ricky ask the
______________________________?
coach to let him play.)

Ricky: No, I can't do that.

MAKING A CONVERSATION

Write a conversation with your partner. Choose one of the following situations, or try one of your own.

1. Your co-worker told the boss that he/she thought of something, but actually it was your idea. A friend sees that something is bothering you and starts a conversation.

2. For the last few years you have gone on a trip during your vacation with a certain friend. Now this friend has asked another friend, who he/she is less friendly with, to go on a trip with him/her. A family member sees you and asks you what's wrong.

TOPICS FOR DISCUSSION

1. What's the matter with Ricky? What did Dan do that Ricky didn't like? Do you think he was disturbed by what Brenda did, too? How do you think he feels about Brenda?

2. Is Ricky jealous of his brother? Have you ever been jealous? If so, when? Did you admit to being jealous or did you say, "I don't care what he/she does."

3. What things matter to you? Does it matter if you don't sleep eight hours at night/if you miss breakfast? Does it matter to you if your husband/wife/boyfriend/girlfriend has a date with someone else?

UNIT 16

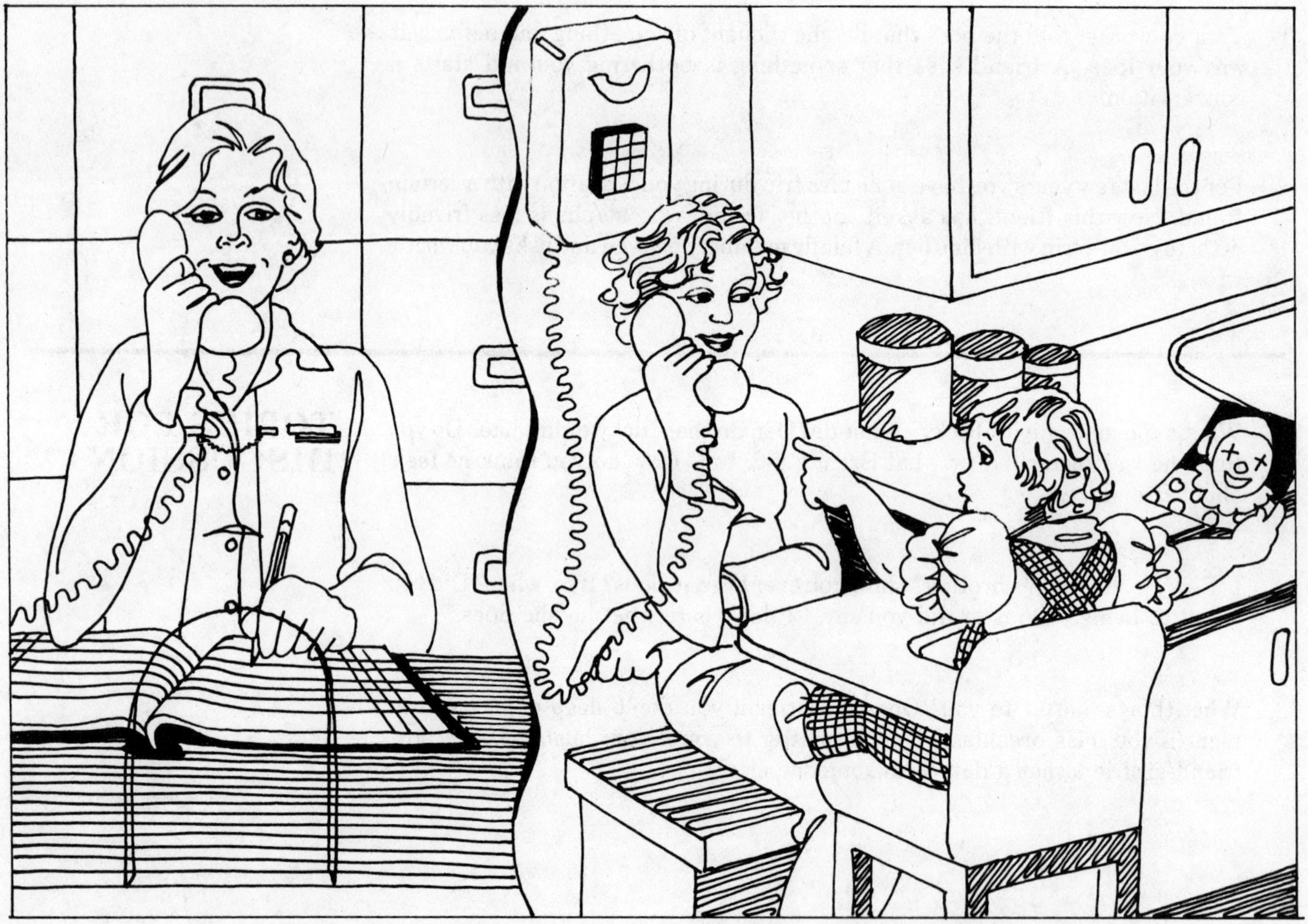

Making an Appointment with the Doctor

Receptionist:	We can give you an appointment this afternoon.
Paula:	You can?
Receptionist:	Yes. We just had a cancellation for 3:45. Would that time be convenient for you?
Paula:	Yes. Lisa should be up long before then.
Receptionist:	Okay. I'll put you down for a quarter to four.
Paula:	Thank you . . . Uh—do you think we'll have to wait long?
Receptionist:	I don't know. You could call up around three to check.
Paula:	Okay, I will.

SPIN-OFF DIALOGUE

Receptionist: I can give you an appointment for 3:45 today.

Paula: At 3:45 today?

Receptionist: Yes. Somebody just made a cancellation. Could you come in then?

Paula: Well, I think so. Lisa gets up from her nap about 2:30.

Receptionist: All right. I'll put you down for a quarter of four.

Paula: Thank you. Do you think there'll be a long wait?

Receptionist: I can't say. You could call up before you leave to check.

Paula: All right. I'll do that.

USEFUL EXPRESSIONS

Asking for Confirmation: (Speaker A) We can give you an appointment this afternoon.
(Speaker B) *You can?*

Asking about Certainty: *Do you think* (that) we'll have to wait long?

Expressing Obligation: We *have to* wait.

Expressing Certainty: *I think so.*

VOCABULARY

NOUNS
cancellation
complex
mechanic
nap
pediatrician
pump
snack
wait

ADJECTIVE
convenient

VERBS
check
drop off
get up
put down
repair
sew
wait

PREPOSITION
around

IDIOMS AND PHRASES
to be up (awake)
wait long
a quarter *to* or *of* the hour

PRACTICE I

1. Fill in the blanks with the correct word(s). Read the paragraph first.

Paula Spock called up the doctor's office to ___make___ (1) an appointment for her daughter, Lisa. It was time for her year-old checkup. Paula was very surprised when the receptionist offered to ______ (2) her an appointment that same day. Paula asked the receptionist, "______ (3)?" When the receptionist wanted to know if they could come in at that time, Paula responded,

"I think ______ (4) ." Paula asked if they would have ______ (5) wait a long time. The receptionist couldn't say. So she suggested that Paula call up around three o'clock ______ (6) .

2. Carry out the following instructions.

example: We just had a cancellation. Make a question with a statement plus question intonation.
You did?

1) Your friend is going to return the money he borrowed. Make a question with a statement plus question intonation.
2) Are you ready for your trip this weekend? Answer that you think so.
3) Say that you have to study for the test.
4) Ask your teacher if he/she thinks that the classroom is too small.
5) Your friend's sister got married. Make a question with a statement plus question intonation.
6) Are you going to wait an hour for Jane and Peter? Answer that you think so.
7) Ask your friend if he thinks he'll cancel his appointment.
8) Say that Linda is obligated to work late tonight.

STRUCTURES

A. Present Modal—SHOULD (Expectation in the Present or in the Future)

Lisa *should* be up about 2:30.
(Her mother expects her to be up then. She generally gets up at that time.)

B. Modal—COULD (Possibility in the Present or in the Future)

You *could* call up around three to check.

C. Future Adverbial Clauses of Time

Before Paula leaves, she'll call the doctor's office.
or, Paula will call the doctor's office *before she leaves.*

We also use *after, when,* and *until* to introduce an adverbial time clause. We use the present tense in the adverbial time clause and the future in the main clause.

PRACTICE II

1. Choose the correct word to complete these sentences.

examples: The two boys aren't sure what to do after school. They **should/could** play in the park.
They could play in the park.

My classmate is a good student. She **should/could** know the answer to this easy question.
She should know the answer to this easy question.

1) I am almost done with this letter. I **should/could** finish it in a few minutes.
2) Sometimes Paula Spock's pediatrician is late for her appointments. The doctor **should/could** be late this afternoon.
3) Lisa generally has a snack after her nap. She **should/could** have her snack about a quarter to three.
4) We don't have plans for our vacation. We **should/could** go to Canada or just stay home this year.
5) They usually get up at seven o'clock. It's seven-thirty. They **should/could** be up now.
6) You don't have all the information. You **shouldn't/couldn't** know what really happened.
7) He made a few big mistakes when he started. But now he understands the job. He **shouldn't/couldn't** have any more problems.
8) I'm not sure about some of my friend's ideas. She **should/could** be wrong.

2. Combine these sentences with the adverbial clause marker.

example: You'll clean your apartment. You'll go out. (before)
You'll clean your apartment before you go out.

1) She'll make an appointment with the boss. She'll get to the office. (after)
2) Tom will buy a box of cookies. He'll go shopping. (when)
3) They'll carry their suitcases. They'll get tired. (until)
4) He'll ask Barbara out. He'll see her. (when)
5) I'll talk to them. I'll make up my mind. (before)
6) We'll stay inside. It'll stop raining. (until)
7) They'll try to spell the word themselves. You'll look it up in your dictionary. (before)
8) It'll be convenient to talk to you. They'll leave. (after)

TRANSFER

1. You are talking to a mechanic at a garage. You want her/him to repair your car. Read the dialogue first; then fill in the blanks with appropriate phrases or sentences.

Mechanic: I can repair your car this morning.

Student: ______________________________?
(With a declarative sentence, ask if she/he can.)

Mechanic: Yes. It doesn't look too difficult. I just have to replace the water pump.

Student: ______________________________?
(Ask if that's all.)

Mechanic: Yes. Do you want to pick up your car about 11:30?

Student: Okay. ______________________________
(Ask if he/she thinks it might be ready sooner.)
______________________________?

Mechanic: It's very possible. You could give us a call around 10:00 to see.

Student: ______________________________.

2. You are talking on the telephone to a receptionist at a large dry cleaners. Read the dialogue first; then fill in the blanks with appropriate words or phrases.

Receptionist: We can have your suit cleaned by five o'clock this afternoon.

Student: ______________________________?
(With a declarative sentence, ask if they can.)

Receptionist: Yes. We offer same-day service.

Student: ______________________________.

Receptionist: Why don't you drop off your suit as soon as you can, and then pick it up at five?

Student: All right. ______________________________
(Ask if he/she thinks they could sew on a few buttons too.)
______________________________?

Receptionist: Yes. Put the buttons in one of the pockets.

Student: ______________________________.

MAKING A CONVERSATION

Write a conversation with your partner. Choose one of the following situations, or try one of your own.

1. You are talking on the telephone to a receptionist at a hair stylist's salon. You want an appointment that afternoon. She says they can give you an appointment at 6:30 because they just had a cancellation. That time is convenient for you, and she puts you down for it. When you ask if there'll be a wait, she answers that she doesn't think so.

2. You are talking on the telephone to a rental agent for an apartment complex. You want to look at a one-bedroom apartment. The rental agent says that he can show you one today and asks if 1:30 would be convenient. You agree and then ask if he thinks you could come in at 1:00 instead. He agrees formally.

TOPICS FOR DISCUSSION

1. Who did Paula make an appointment with? Who was it for? Why? Do you have medical checkups every year? Why or why not?

2. When could the receptionist give her an appointment? Why? Was Paula surprised? Is it usual or unusual to see a doctor right away for a checkup?

3. Is 3:45 a convenient time for Lisa's appointment? Why? In certain parts of the world shops and businesses close in the middle of the day and adults take a nap. What are normal business hours in your country?

4. Does the receptionist think Paula and Lisa will have a long wait? What does she say that Paula could do? Do you think that Paula likes to wait in the doctor's waiting room? How long do you usually have to wait to see the doctor? What are some reasons why there's sometimes a long wait for a doctor's appointment?

UNIT 17

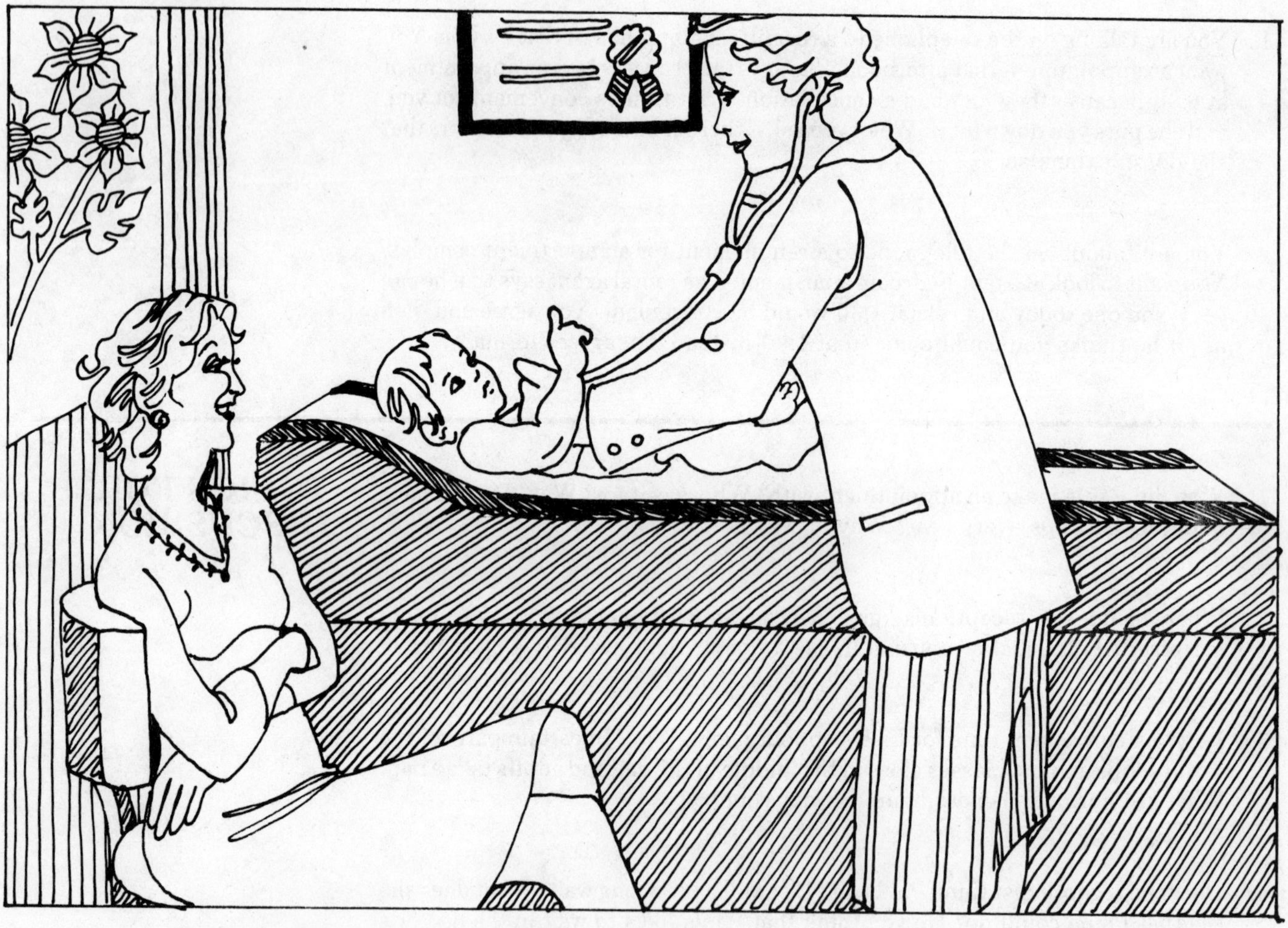

In the Examining Room

Dr. Jacobs: Lisa is in perfect health.

Paula: That's good. I'm delighted.

Dr. Jacobs: Have you had any problems at all with her?

Paula: No . . . except I'm a little worried that she hasn't started to stand up yet.

Dr. Jacobs: That's completely normal. Standing comes before walking. But some babies don't walk until they're a year and a half.

Paula: I was wondering if there was anything I could do to speed up the process.

Dr. Jacobs: No, not really. When Lisa is ready, she'll stand up, then side-step holding onto furniture, and then walk.

SPIN-OFF DIALOGUE

Dr. Jacobs:	Lisa is in excellent health.
Paula:	That's great.
Dr. Jacobs:	Any problems?
Paula:	No . . . only, is it all right that she isn't standing up yet?
Dr. Jacobs:	Yes. Babies all develop differently. They stand before they walk. But some don't walk until sixteen months or later.
Paula:	Is there anything I could do to speed up the process?
Dr. Jacobs:	No. When Lisa is ready, she'll start by herself. And once she begins walking, you won't be able to stop her.

USEFUL EXPRESSIONS

Expressing Fear or Worry:	*I'm worried* (that) . . . .
Asking for Approval:	*Is it all right that . . . ?* *Is that all right?* *Is this okay?*
Expressing Inability:	You *won't be able to* stop her. (future)

VOCABULARY

NOUNS
furniture
health
hygienist
insurance
nursery school
process

ADJECTIVES
delighted
excellent
normal
perfect
ready
sensitive
worried

ADVERBS
completely
differently
once

VERBS
be able to
develop
hold
limit
side-step
speed up
stand
stand up
wonder

PREPOSITION
onto

IDIOMS AND PHRASES
by oneself (= alone)
not really

PRACTICE I

1. *Correct or Incorrect.* **If the following statements are correct, say, "That's correct." If they are incorrect, say, "That's incorrect." Then make the statements correct.**

examples: You are not certain if you are able to play the last part of a piece of music again. You say to your piano teacher, "I was wondering if I could play the last part again." <u>That's correct.</u>

You play the last part again and then ask for your piano teacher's approval. "Was it bad this time?" <u>That's not correct. You should say, "Was it all right this time?"</u> or, <u>"Was it okay this time?"</u>

1) They can't carry out your instructions. They express their inability and say, "We aren't able to carry out your instructions."
2) You express your worry that you'll miss the boat. You say, "I'm worried that I'll miss the boat."
3) The boy's mother says that she is not very certain that he cleaned up his room. She says, "I think he cleaned up his room."
4) I'm incapable of swimming to the other side of the pool. I'm able to swim to the other side of the pool.
5) You ask your English teacher's approval of your answer to her question and say, "Was my answer good?"
6) Your friend is very sick. You express your worry that he might have to go to the hospital. You say, "I'm worried that he might have to go to the hospital."
7) Nancy's classmates say that they are not very certain Nancy solved the problem. One of them says, "We were wondering if you solved the problem."
8) You ask your friend's approval of your dress for the party. You say, "Is this dress all right?"

2. **Fill in the blanks with the correct word(s).**

example: I'm <u>worried</u> my car will run out of gas.

1) Is it all __________ if he comes with us?
2) Lisa isn't __________ to walk yet.
3) I __________ if that's "normal."
4) Was it __________ right to tell them what I really thought?
5) I'll __________ worried if you don't call me.
6) Mr. Stone won't be able __________ repair the radio by himself.
7) We were wondering __________ they were locked out.
8) She __________ worried after she spoke to him.

STRUCTURES

A. Gerunds and Gerund Phrases as Subjects

Standing comes before walking.
Side-stepping along furniture also comes before walking.

B. Count Nouns and Mass Nouns without *The*

Babies develop differently. (Count Noun)
Some parents prefer *girls;* others prefer *boys.* (Count Nouns)
All children need *love.* (Mass Noun)

We use plural count nouns and singular mass nouns without *the* when we are making general statements.

PRACTICE II

1. Change these sentences so that a gerund phrase is the subject.

example: It's important to come to school on time.
Coming to school on time is important.

1) It was easy to learn those words.
2) It's expensive to move to a distant state.
3) It was a good idea to invite his brother.
4) It's sometimes hard to make new friends.
5) It's normal to think like that.
6) It's impossible to speed up the process.
7) It was a pleasure to talk with them.
8) It was all right to change your plans.

2. Make general statements with these cue words.

examples: ice Ice is cold.
cars Cars have wheels.

1) carrots
2) trees
3) sugar
4) houses
5) pens
6) babies
7) snow
8) balls

TRANSFER

1. Dr. Jacobs is talking to the mother of a three-year-old boy. Read the dialogue first; then fill in the blanks with appropriate phrases or sentences.

Dr. Jacobs: Patrick is a very healthy boy.

Student: ______________________________.
(Express approval.)

Dr. Jacobs: Have you had any problems with him at all?

Student: ________. ______________________________
(Say there is one. Patrick just started nursery school, and he cries
____
when you leave him there.)
______________________________.

Dr. Jacobs: That happens with some children. It takes them a while to adjust to a new situation and to being away from you.

Student: ______________________________
(Ask if there's anything you can do to make it easier for Patrick.)
______________________________?

Dr. Jacobs: You could stay with him at the nursery school until he feels comfortable and seems to forget you're there.

2. Dr. Jacobs is talking to the father of a nine-year-old girl. Read the dialogue first; then fill in the blanks with appropriate phrases or sentences.

Dr. Jacobs: Laura is in excellent health.

Student: ______________________________.
(Express approval.)

Dr. Jacobs: Any problems with her?

Student: ______________________________.
(Say, "No . . . just that Laura watches a lot of television every day.
______________________________?
Is that all right?")

Dr. Jacobs: No, I don't think so. Laura needs to be with other children.

Student: ______________________________?
(Ask what you should do.)

Dr. Jacobs: You could limit her TV watching to the evening. And ask her to invite a friend to play at your house after school.

MAKING A CONVERSATION

Write a conversation with your partner. Choose one of the following situations, or try one of your own.

1. You are talking to an insurance agent about your policy. Everything is in order. You express approval. Then she asks if you have any questions. You ask her if it's all right if you mail your first check in next month. She says it should be. Then you ask her when you'll begin to be covered by your policy. She answers you.

2. You are talking to the dentist after the dental hygienist cleaned your teeth. He tells you that your teeth are in very good condition. You express approval. Then he asks you if you've had any problems. You tell him that one tooth hurts after you eat something hot. He tells you that's not serious. That tooth is sensitive to hot things. Then you ask him if there's anything you could do. The dentist suggests you try a certain kind of toothpaste. It should help.

TOPICS FOR DISCUSSION

1. How was Lisa's checkup? Is she in perfect health? How is your health?

2. Does Paula have any problems with her daughter? What is she a little worried about? Should she be worried? Why or why not? Is anybody in your family worried about you? If somebody is, what is he/she worried about? Should he/she be worried? Why or why not?

3. Do babies all develop differently? What do they do before they walk? At what age do some babies begin to walk? When will Lisa start to walk by herself? Will Paula be able to stop her once she begins? Do you think Paula is impatient about Lisa's starting to walk? Why? Are you impatient about anything now? If you are, what is it? When are you patient?

UNIT 18

At a Bar

Waiter: Are you ready to order?

Dan: Yes. I'll have a beer. Make it Shaff's.

Brenda: Er, uh. I'll have a Coke. I guess. *(The waiter leaves.)* Dan, why did you take me here?

Dan: I don't know. I thought you might like to see what a college-type bar was like.

Brenda: But I don't drink. And besides I shouldn't be here. My mother wouldn't like it.

Dan: You sound like a little girl.

Brenda: Well, I am only fifteen. We shouldn't have come here. Please take me home.

Dan: Look, Brenda, I'm sorry. We're leaving right now . . . Waiter!

SPIN-OFF DIALOGUE

Waiter: What'll it be, folks?

Dan: I'll have a rum and Coke.

Brenda: Uh, I'd like a glass of . . . ginger ale. *(The waiter goes away.)* How come you brought me here, Dan?

Dan: Well, I thought you'd enjoy yourself. This bar is one of the most popular around.

Brenda: But I don't drink. And besides if my mother knew I was here, she wouldn't like it at all.

Dan: Come on, Brenda, relax. You're not giving this place a chance.

Brenda: Well, I don't want to. We shouldn't have come. I wish you'd take me home.

Dan: Okay, okay. We're going right now . . . Waiter!

USEFUL EXPRESSIONS

Expressing Desire: I'*d like* a glass of ginger ale.

Expressing Disapproval: I *shouldn't be* here.
(+ verb)
We *shouldn't have come* here.
(+ past participle)

Making a Request: *Please take me home.*
(+ verb or verb phrase)

VOCABULARY

NOUNS
acquaintance
bar
beer
chance
Coke
ginger ale
lie
rum
waitress

ADJECTIVES
popular
thirsty

ADVERB
besides

VERBS
brought (bring)
enjoy oneself
give
order
wish

IDIOMS AND PHRASES
around
folks (= people)
give something/someone a chance
how come (= why)
right now
sound
what something/someone is like

PRACTICE I

1. Put these words in the correct order to make sentences.

example: beer like a he'd .
He'd like a beer.

1) me please home take .
2) have here we come shouldn't .
3) ale glass I'd a ginger of like .
4) bar thinks at shouldn't Brenda the be she .
5) waiter the call please .
6) Dan taken there Brenda have shouldn't .
7) like to home go I'd .
8) talking they leave the without to waiter shouldn't .

2. Carry out the following instructions.

example: You were late for work. Express your boss's disapproval.
You shouldn't have been late.

1) Your class is beginning now. But you are still home. Express a member of your family's disapproval.
2) Request that your friend listen to you.
3) You are at a restaurant. Say that you want a clean fork.
4) Your friend believed a lie about you. Express disapproval.
5) Request that your classmate lend you a pencil.
6) Say that you want to relax for a little while.
7) Your co-worker wants to leave the meeting now. Express disapproval.
8) You changed your answer on the test. Express disapproval.

STRUCTURES

A. Conditional with an *If*-Clause (Present Time)

If my mother *knew,* she *wouldn't like* it.

This is contrary-to-fact because she doesn't know.

Dan *would buy* a new motorcycle if he *had* more money.
(He'*d*)

This is contrary-to-fact because he doesn't have more money.

We use the past tense in the *if*-clause and *would* + verb in the main clause to express a situation that is not real at the present time.

B. Future Noun Clauses after *Wish*

Dan *wishes* **Brenda would relax.**
Brenda *wishes* **he'd take her home.**
The waiter *wishes* **they wouldn't leave.**

When a clause after the *wish*-clause refers to the future, we use *would* + verb. The subject of the second clause is usually different from the subject of the *wish*-clause.

PRACTICE II

1. Answer these questions with present conditionals.

example: What would you do if you found $100?
If I found $100, I'd put it in the bank.

1) What would you do if you lost your wallet?
2) What would you do if you couldn't understand the lesson?
3) Where would you go if you could take a trip?
4) What would you do if you went to a party where you didn't know anybody?
5) What would you do if your best friend needed help?
6) What would you do if somebody you didn't like asked for your help?
7) What would you say if you wanted someone to be quiet?
8) What would you do if your watch stopped working?

2. Make new sentences with the *wish*-clauses.

example: You won't smoke. (I wish)
I wish you wouldn't smoke.

1) The weather will change. (She wishes)
2) They won't play that song. (I wish)
3) She'll go on a diet. (You wish)
4) His car will start. (He wishes)
5) Their parents will take them to the parade. (The children wish)
6) He won't bother her. (She wishes)
7) The teacher will give them more time to do the assignment. (The students wish)
8) You won't talk like that. (I wish)

TRANSFER

1. You are at a wild party with Brenda. Read the dialogue first; then fill in the blanks with appropriate phrases or sentences.

Student: ____?
(Ask if she wants some wine.)

Brenda: No, thank you. I don't drink. Tell me, why did you bring me here?

Student: ____.
(Say you thought she might enjoy herself.)

Brenda: I really shouldn't be here. If my mother knew I was here, she wouldn't like it at all.

Student: ____
(Tell her she's not giving the party a chance.)
____.

Brenda: Well, I don't want to. You shouldn't have brought me here. Please take me home.

Student: ____________ . ______________________________
(Say, "All right. Look, Brenda, I'm sorry. We're leaving right now.")
____.

2. You are at a football game with Dan. Read the dialogue first; then fill in the blanks with appropriate words or phrases.

Dan: Do you want me to get you something to drink?

Student: ____________________ . ____________________
(Say, "No thanks." You're not thirsty. Ask him why he brought you
____?
here.)

Dan: I thought you might like to see our school team play.

Student: ____.
(Say, but you don't like football. And besides, you've never
____
understood how it is played and never will.)
____.

Dan: Come on, ____________ . You're not giving the game a chance.
(your name)

Student: ____________________ . ____________________.
(Say, well you don't want to. We shouldn't have come . . .
____.
Let's go some place else.)

Dan: Okay, okay. We're leaving right now.

MAKING A CONVERSATION

Write a conversation with your partner. Choose one of the following situations, or try one of your own.

1. An acquaintance takes you to a Chinese restaurant where they only serve very hot, spicy food. He orders something spicy; you ask your companion why he brought you here. He answers that he thought you might enjoy that kind of Chinese food. But you reply that you don't like very spicy food. He tells you to relax and to give the place a chance. You refuse and express disapproval and then suggest going to a different restaurant. He agrees and calls the waiter.

2. A friend takes you to an opera for the first time. She asks you if you want her to tell you what it's about. You answer, "All right." Then you ask her why she brought you here. She answers that she thought that you might like to see a famous opera. You answer that you don't like opera, and besides you can't understand a word they're saying. Finish the conversation yourself.

TOPICS FOR DISCUSSION

1. Where did Dan take Brenda on their date? Do you think this is a good place for a first date? Why or why not? Where would you suggest going on a first date?

2. What did Dan order? What did Brenda order? Did each of them give their order separately to the waiter? In America sometimes a woman orders for herself if she is with a man, or sometimes he orders for her. In your country of origin, does a woman give her order herself, or does the man she is with order for her?

3. Does Brenda think she should be at the bar? If Brenda's mother knew she was there, would she like it? How old is Brenda? Do you think she is too young to be at a bar? Why or why not? What is the legal age for drinking where you live now? In your country?

4. Do you think Dan enjoyed himself? Why or why not? Do you think Brenda enjoyed herself? Why or why not? If you went to a college-type bar, would you enjoy yourself? Why or why not?

UNIT
19

Meeting Someone by Chance

Carol: Hello, Harry!

Harry: Hi! *(He stops to talk to her.)*

Carol: How's your jogging coming along?

Harry: Fine. I just ran a quarter of a mile. Not too fast, of course. I jog now every day except if it rains . . . How're you doing?

Carol: Okay. I started a diet two weeks ago. Can you see I've lost about ten pounds?

Harry: Yes, I can. How much do you want to lose?

Carol: Oh, about twenty-five pounds.

SPIN-OFF DIALOGUE

Carol: Hi!

Harry: Carol! *(He stops to chat.)*

Carol: How're you doing with your jogging?

Harry: Very well. I jog every day now unless it rains. And then I go to the "Y." How're things with you?

Carol: Okay. I went on a diet two weeks ago. And this time it's working. So far, I've lost about ten pounds.

Harry: Yes, I can *see.* How much more do you want to lose?

Carol: Around thirty pounds.

USEFUL EXPRESSIONS

Responding to a Greeting:	*How're (How are) things (with you)?* (informal) *Fine.* (response) *Okay.* (response)
Asking about Ability:	*Can* you see I've lost about ten pounds?
Expressing Ability:	I *can.* I *can* see.

VOCABULARY

NOUNS
athlete
goal
diet
lap
mile
pound
quarter

VERBS
come along
jog
knit
lost (lose)
ran (run)

PREPOSITIONS
except

SUBORDINATING CONJUNCTION
unless

IDIOMS AND PHRASES
by chance
get out of shape
How are (How're) things?
How's your ______ coming along?
stand on one's head
work (= be successful)

PRACTICE I

1. *Correct or Incorrect.* If the following statements are correct, say, "That's correct." If they are incorrect, say, "That's incorrect." Then make the statements correct.

examples: You respond to your boss's wife's greeeting by saying, "Fine, thank you." <u>That's correct.</u>

Your friend responds to your greeting saying, "How do you do?" <u>That's incorrect. He says, "Hi," or, "Hello."</u>

1) Somebody asks if you can smell the cake in the oven. You answer, "Yes, I can."
2) An old classmate and you begin to chat. You ask him, "What time is it?" He answers you and says, "Okay."
3) You inquire about a family member's ability to stand on her head. You ask, "Can she stand on your head?"
4) You introduce a friend to your grandmother and your friend says, "How are things?"
5) An athlete talks about his jogging ability. He says, "I might jog five miles a day."
6) You ask a tourist how many languages she's capable of speaking. "How many languages can you speak?"
7) The telephone is ringing. You answer it and greet the person on the other end. You say, "Hi."

2. Fill in the blanks with the correct word.

Harry Mullens met Carol Wright while he was <u>jogging</u> (1). He stopped ____________ (2) chat with her. Harry said that he jogged every day ____________ (3) if it ____________ (4). And then he would go to ____________ (5) "Y." Carol told Harry that she started a ____________ (6) two weeks ago. Then she asked him, "____________ (7) you see I've lost about ten pounds?" He answered that he could and asked her how much ____________ (8) she wanted to lose. Carol answered, "____________ (9) twenty-five pounds."

STRUCTURES

A. *Unless*

I jog every day *unless* it rains.
I jog every day *except if* it rains.

We use *unless* to mean *except if. Unless* indicates a condition is necessary in order to change the situation in the main clause.

B. Noun Clauses as Direct Objects with and without *That*

Can you see *that I've lost about ten pounds*?
He noticed *she had lost some weight.*

That is the first word in some noun clauses. We never put a comma between the main verb and *that.*

PRACTICE II

1. Make new sentences with *unless* and the information in the cue sentences.

example: Jack won't go to the party. (You must go, too.)
Jack won't go to the party unless you go.

1) I can't move the furniture. (I must get some help.)
2) Carol won't lose any more weight. (She must stay on her diet.)
3) Don't use the copying machine. (You must have permission.)
4) You won't get over your cold. (You must take your medicine.)
5) He'll wait outside for you. (It must be very cold.)
6) They call their mother every Sunday on the telephone. (They must be away from home.)
7) The doctor can't give you a checkup this week. (There must be a cancellation.)
8) Please don't tell them anything. (You must trust them.)

2. Make sentences with the noun clauses in this list. You may use one item more than once.

they're going to buy a new house
he lost his job
she was wrong
I spent my vacation in California
we joined the club
you didn't sleep well
today was Thursday

1) Did you hear (that)
2) He told me (that)
3) We can see (that)
4) I thought (that)
5) Do they know (that)
6) She said (that)
7) Our friends think (that)
8) You didn't know (that)

TRANSFER

1. **You work at the bank with Carol. You are trying to improve your typing. Read the dialogue first; then fill in the blanks with appropriate phrases or sentences.**

Carol: Hi!

Student: ______________________________ .
(Greet Carol.) (She stops to chat.)

Carol: How's your typing coming along?

Student: ______________ . ______________
(Tell her very well. You practice every day if there's not too much work.

______________________________ .

______________________________ ?
Ask how things are with her.)

Carol: Fine. I got a new chair, and it's much more comfortable than the old one. Can you see it over there? *(She points to it.)*

Student: __________ . ______________________
(Answer with a positive short answer.

__________ . ______________________ ?
Ask her with a tag question if it isn't too high for her desk.)

Carol: No, it's just right.

2. **You meet Harry at the YMCA. He's swimming in the pool. Read the dialogue first; then fill in the blanks with appropriate phrases or sentences.**

Student: ______________________________ .
(Greet Harry.)

Harry: Hi.

Student: ______________________________
(Ask how he's doing with his physical fitness program.)

______________________________ ?

Harry: Fine. But I've found unless I keep at it every day, I get out of shape. How are you doing?

Student: __________ . ______________________ .
(Say, "Fine." Tell him you can now swim fifteen laps in the pool.

______________________ . __________
Tell him to watch this.) (You swim a short distance.) (Ask him how

______________________________ ?
that was.)

Harry: Good. Just try to raise your left arm some more.

MAKING A CONVERSATION

Write a conversation with your partner. Choose one of the following situations, or try one of your own.

1. You are painting a picture. A friend sees you and asks how it's coming along. You answer him, and then say you paint a little every day unless you are too busy with other things. Then you ask him how things are going with him. He tells you that he's started to take guitar lessons. You ask him if he can play any songs yet.

2. You are knitting a scarf. A relative asks you how you are doing with it. You reply and then say you always knit a little every day unless you're very tired. Then you ask her how she is doing with her sewing. She tells you that she just made a dress. You ask if you can see it sometime. She answers that you can see it right now because she's wearing it.

TOPICS FOR DISCUSSION

1. Who did Carol meet by chance? What was he doing? What did he stop to do? Have you met anyone by chance recently? If you have, describe the circumstances.

2. How is Harry's jogging coming along? How often does he jog? Where does he go sometimes?

3. Do you think what Harry is doing is good for him? Do you ever go jogging? If you don't, do you do other physical exercise regularly? If you do, what is it? Do you think physical exercise is important? Why or why not?

4. What did Carol do two weeks ago? Can Harry see that she has lost weight? How much weight has she lost so far? How much more does she want to lose?

5. Carol's goal is that she wants to lose a certain amount of weight. Are you trying to reach a personal goal now? If you are, what is it? How are you coming along? If you aren't trying to reach a personal goal now, have you ever tried to improve something about yourself in the past? If you have, what was it?

UNIT 20

Saying Good Night

Mrs. Climo: Shouldn't you be in bed? It's past midnight.

Ricky: Oh, is it? I thought it was still only about eleven.

Mrs. Climo: Haven't you finished all your homework yet?

Ricky: Yes, hours ago. I was just doing some extra reading for my science project.

Mrs. Climo: Well, that's enough now. Remember tomorrow is a school day.

Ricky: All right. I'll go to bed as soon as I finish this page.

Mrs. Climo: Good night, dear. Sleep well.

Ricky: Good night, Mom.

SPIN-OFF DIALOGUE

Mrs. Climo: Ricky, do you know it's after twelve o'clock?

Ricky: No. I completely forgot about the time.

Mrs. Climo: Are you still doing your homework?

Ricky: No, this book is for my science project. My chemistry teacher lent it to me.

Mrs. Climo: Well, you've done enough reading for one night. Remember you have school tomorrow.

Ricky: Okay. I'll turn off the light as soon as I'm done with this section.

Mrs. Climo: All right. Good night.

Ricky: Good night.

USEFUL EXPRESSIONS

Reminding Someone: *Remember* tomorrow is a school day.
(noun clause)
Remember to set your alarm clock.
(infinitive phrase)

Forgetting: *I forgot* about the time.
I forgot to look at my watch.
(infinitive phrase)

Taking Leave: *Good night.*

VOCABULARY

NOUNS
chemistry
florist
light
page
project
reading
science
section

ADJECTIVE
extra

ADVERB
completely

VERBS
forgot (forget)
lent (lend)
sleep
turn off

PREPOSITION
past

IDIOMS AND PHRASES
as soon as
do homework (work of any kind)
go to bed
in bed

PRACTICE I

1. Fill in the blanks with the correct word(s).

example: She can't open the door. She forgot her key.

1) Before the little boy went to bed, he said ____________ to his parents.
2) You may borrow my notebook, but please remember ____________ return it before the weekend.
3) What's your name again? I'm sorry I ____________ it.
4) I told my friend, "____________," and shut off the lights.
5) ____________ tonight we're going out for dinner. Don't eat a big lunch.
6) I always forget ____________ lock my suitcase. One day something might get stolen.

2. Carry out the following instructions.

example: "We've already made plans." Ask a short question. Begin with "oh."

Oh, have you?

1) They can type very fast. Ask a short question. Begin with "oh."
2) Tell someone to remember to do something before he goes out.
3) Take leave of a family member before going to bed.
4) State that you have forgotten to bring something to school.
5) You know those people over there. Ask a short question. Begin with "oh."
6) Say that you completely forgot about your appointment with the doctor, the dentist, or the lawyer.
7) She still has to do her homework. Ask a short question. Begin with "oh."
8) Tell a classmate to remember something about tomorrow.

STRUCTURES

A. Direct Objects and Indirect Objects

The teacher *lent*	***Ricky*** (indirect object)	**a book.** (direct object)
The teacher *lent*	***him*** (indirect object)	**a book** (direct object)

When the direct object is a noun, we put it *after* the indirect object. The indirect object can be a noun or a pronoun.

The teacher *lent*	**it**	to ***him/Ricky.***
	(direct object)	(indirect object)

When the direct object is a pronoun, we put it *before* the indirect object. Then we put the indirect object in a prepositional phrase with *to* or *for.*

The following verbs take *to* with indirect objects: *give, lend, send, tell,* and *write.* The following verbs take *for* with indirect objects: *buy, do,* and *make.*

B. *Enough*

	Enough +	Noun +	Prepositional Phrase
You've done	*enough.*		
You've done	*enough*	**reading.**	
You've done	*enough*	**reading**	***for one night.***

	Enough +	Noun +	Infinitive (Phrase)
They had	*enough*	**time**	***to finish (it).***

We generally put *enough* before nouns. After the nouns we sometimes put a prepositional phrase or an infinitive (phrase).

PRACTICE II

1. Change the noun indirect objects to pronouns in a prepositional phrase in the following sentences.

examples: Please give Mary the book.
Please give the book to her.

Can you buy Charles this coat?
Can you buy this coat for him?

1) Don't lend Elizabeth your pencil.
2) She wants to send her brother these pictures.
3) You must tell Mr. and Mrs. Small the story.
4) I've already given you and your secretary the information.
5) We made Stanley some bookshelves.
6) Please do your mother a favor.
7) They wrote my friend and me a letter.
8) He plans to buy his wife this necklace.

2. Put these words in the correct order to make sentences.

example: weekend food have enough the we for .
We have enough food for the weekend.

1) for are chairs the enough there meeting .
2) time I enough walk the have theater to to .
3) test studied for she's enough the .
4) you enough party the bought for wine .
5) to car they money enough new a buy have .
6) in room his has apartment he enough .
7) enough mother he's one thinks done Ricky's reading night for .
8) game that to have people we play enough card .

TRANSFER

1. You have a part-time job at a florist's in addition to your evening English classes. One evening Mrs. Climo sees you working in the store. Read the dialogue first; then fill in the blanks with appropriate phrases or sentences.

Mrs. Climo: Shouldn't you be in school now? It's seven o'clock.

Student: ________ ? ______________________ .
(Ask if it is. Then say you thought it was still only about six.)

Mrs. Climo: Have you finished all your work here?

Student: ______________________________ .
(Say, "Yes," that you were just cleaning up for tomorrow.

______________________________ .
Your boss, Mrs. Peres, has already gone home for the day.)

Mrs. Climo: Then why don't you close up the store now and hurry over to school?

Student: ______________________________
(Say you think you'll close up now; but then

______________________________ .
you're going home.)

Mrs. Climo: You are?

Student: ________ . ______________________ .
(Say, "Yes." You don't have school on Tuesdays.)

2. You see Ricky in a coffee shop. He is writing something in a notebook. It's getting late. Read the dialogue first; then fill in the blanks with appropriate phrases or sentences.

Student: ______________________________ ?
(Ask if Ricky knows it's almost nine-thirty.)

Ricky: No. My watch stopped.

Student: ____?
(Ask what he's doing.)

Ricky: Oh, this? I've just been writing down some thoughts about . . . something.

Student: ____
(Say that you see. Tell him you'll see him tomorrow . . .
____.
Good night.)

Ricky: Good night.

MAKING A CONVERSATION

Write a conversation with your partner. Choose one of the following situations, or try one of your own.

1. You see a neighbor's daughter playing near your apartment/house. You ask her what kind of toy she's playing with. She tells you. Then you say that's enough for now, and tell her it's dinner-time. She starts to go. You tell her to remember to look both ways before she crosses the street.

2. You are an overnight guest at a friend's home. He/she sees you are still watching TV. He/she asks you if you know it's one o'clock in the morning. You answer that you completely forgot about the time. Then he/she asks you if the movie is almost finished. You answer "yes" and that you'll turn off the TV when it's over. You say good night to each other. He/she tells you to sleep well.

TOPICS FOR DISCUSSION

1. Why does Mrs. Climo think Ricky should be in bed? What time are you usually in bed on weekdays/on weekends? Did Ricky forget about the time? Was he still doing his homework? When did he finish it? What time do you usually finish your homework?

2. Who lent Ricky the book he was reading? Has anybody lent you a book recently? If somebody has, what is the book? Are you still reading it?

3. Does Mrs. Climo think Ricky has done enough reading for one night? What does his mother tell him to remember? When will Ricky go to bed? What kind of student do you think Ricky is? Why? Do you ever stay up late studying?

4. When was the last time you completely forgot about the time? What were you doing? Do you ever forget about the time when you are in school? If you do, describe the circumstances.